Gubbo,
You have no idea
how much I love
you! You are so much my
3 (living). Thank you for your
and support-
love you

MILLIONAIRE
M.O.M.

Living Dreams,
Transforming Lives, and
Defying the Odds of Teen Motherhood

Foreword written by
Tanya Winfield

Dorothea Cooper

Melanie Foote-Davis

Sylvia Duncan

Conchetta Jones

Corita Key

Luberta Lytle

Chandra Pointer

Dr. Catrina Pullum

LaKeisha Stringfellow

Shettima Webb

Alicia T. Bowens

Millionaire M.O.M.

Cover design by Sandra Ballenger (www.sandraballenger.com)

Published by 220 Publishing
(A division of 220 Communications)
P.O. Box 8186
Chicago, IL 60680-8186
www.220communications.com
www.twitter.com/220Comm

ISBN 978-1-513611-84-6

Dedication

This book is dedicated to my two *Why's* – Aamir and Jaden. You both motivate me to be better, do better, and be the example of success for you.

Foreword by Tanya Winfield

How can an Unplanned Pregnancy bring forth Planned Purpose!?

In my era, Teenage Mothers were shunned, ridiculed, isolated, and labeled with a stigma of living in poverty. We were made to feel undesirable, unintelligent, and disadvantaged for life. But what most didn't realize is that we strategically used every brick thrown at us to create a foundation of resilience and a spirit of being unbreakable!

We used our Unplanned Pregnancy to propel us towards Planned Destiny that didn't mirror any of the negative being thrown at us. We became fearless, strong, intelligent, empathic Queens with Children who see us as their Role Models. The Teen Mother who was once belittled and left with feelings of insecurities now encourages, inspires, and instills self-worth in millions of Women on NBC's The Biggest Loser. The Teen Mother who begged for minimum wage entry level jobs, not only became a six-figure income earner as an Executive Leader in Corporate America but is also an Entrepreneur who has employed 100's and pays more than minimum wage. The Teen Mom who was told she would live a life of poverty earned her first million by the age of thirty-five and now mentors other Entrepreneurs and College Students to prevent them from living a life of poverty. The Teen Mother who was told her environment would influence her to become a perpetual victim is now perpetually victorious and influencing her environment. The Teen Mother who once lowered her head in embarrassment and shame became an Honorable Queen who now raises her head amongst the Wealthy, Celebrities, Professionals, and other Elite. The Teen Mom who was told her womb was tainted, has birthed beautiful, God-Fearing, and educated children whose success and potential taunts the Naysayers.

You see, my unplanned pregnancy didn't yield a life with no purpose. My unplanned pregnancy catapulted me into planned destiny. I gave birth to my son at seventeen, but he truly gave me life! I raised a King at seventeen.

This literary masterpiece will not only capture your attention but it will also help you to contextualize your life as a teenage mother so that God is glorified through it.

Author Alicia Bowens, and other Millionaire M.O.M.s through this book, have allowed truth and transparency to be the principles that will lead you to a place of profound perspective in teenage pregnancy. You will not only learn how to deal with it, but you'll discover your destiny through it.

Tanya Winfield, CEO

NBC's Biggest Loser Fan Favorite and Top 6 finalist

Entrepreneur, Motivational Speaker, Corporate Executive Leader, but most importantly the Proud Mother of a King, A Queen, and a Prince

Table of Contents

Introduction

"You have a baby now" are the words that become all too familiar to teen mothers, basically implying that they can forget about their dreams because now their focus should be completely on that child. On top of that, it seems that society has written them off. They're isolated from the "normal" kids as if they have a disease that no one wants to catch, and are made to feel ashamed and unworthy. They want to prove the world wrong and to show them that they can still succeed. However, the level of success attained is often dictated by the amount of support and resources available to them, making it a challenge to do so. Inevitably, the majority resign from their vision of a successful life to merely surviving day to day. They hit the "off" switch to their dreams and identity and go into autopilot in order to live out the expectations and demands placed on them. Mother. Friend. Sibling. Daughter. Wife. Employee. Who has time to dream?

However, today's society is ripe with opportunities for mothers. We are now embraced by the corporate world, as seen by the way they have adopted nursing rooms, in-house childcare, and embraced the importance of work-life balance. More and more of us are breaking barriers, landing major positions in the "C-suite." Entrepreneurship among us is at an all-time high, bringing about the era of the "Mom-preneur." And while teenage pregnancy is still not accepted, it is less taboo, therefore, more resources are available for us young mothers. So, why not dream?

With this new reality, the opportunities are potentially endless. Now there is only one critical thing stopping us from going on to pursue the dreams we once had for our lives, escaping a life of poverty and creating the lives we envisioned for ourselves. That one thing is our mindset.

My experience as a teen mother was full of support from my family and close friends. However, I still devalued myself and my capabilities because being a young mother was not how I expected my life to be. This devaluation caused me to make a lot of poor decisions, which I discuss later on in this book, and only exacerbated my devaluation of self. As a result, the amount of success I achieved was always limited. It was only once I began to once again realize my self-worth and believe that the dreams I had for myself were possible for me, that I began experiencing major breakthroughs in my life.

Every author in this book agrees that her child was

not the major obstacle – her mindset was. Each author shares her experiences and the things that she had to overcome to be successful. I have no doubt that once you read our stories and really apply the lessons that each of us has learned, you will be on your way to success as well!

Who is a Millionaire M.O.M.? Let me help you paint a picture of her: A Millionaire M.O.M. is a Mother On a Mission to realize her greatest self. While she may not necessarily be a millionaire, she knows that a fortune exists within her. She believes she was placed on this earth for a reason and will do what it takes to make sure her purpose is fulfilled. She understands that she is capable of creating the wealth she desires. She realizes that everything she needs to take her life to new levels already exists within her and she invests in herself regularly to uncover and sharpen those skills.

Her experiences growing up may not have been the most ideal, but she refuses to let her past define her. Her children are her motivation to be the example of success that she knows also exists within them. She is on a mission to build a legacy and create wealth for her family that will last for generations to come.

In this volume, you will hear the stories of a number of Millionaire M.O.M.s. These mothers share a similarity that is near and dear to my heart – they all became mothers during their teenage years. I was also one of them. However, we were able to overcome the obstacles associated with teen motherhood. There were a lot of things that we had to overcome, both mentally and physically. There were many truths we had to face and a lot of hard questions we had to ask ourselves in order to identify who we were and what we wanted in life. The one thing that we all understood, and want you to understand, is that change had to begin within us. We had to look beyond our circumstances, the shame, the rejection, the hurt, and make a decision.

We made the decision that our circumstances were not a death sentence for our destiny. We made the decision that the rejection, hurt, and shame we experienced would not determine our worth. Then, most importantly, we took action on things that supported our decisions. We continued our education. We left the toxic relationships behind. We pursued our careers. We started our businesses. We wrote our books. And we did it all afraid – not knowing what would happen, what to do next, and in spite of the fear and naysayers.

When I would go speak to teen mothers at local high schools and organizations, I would often ask them questions in order to learn more about them and their children. I would first ask about their children. Immediately I would see these young mothers' enthusiasm as they explained their children's quirks and personalities. They would go on and on about things their kids did that made them laugh, as well as their likes and dislikes.

Then I would shift gears and ask these same mothers' questions about themselves – questions like what did they like to do, what did they want to be, what were some of their qualities? These questions, unfortunately, were met with a sobering silence, even a few honest replies of "I don't know."

Their responses were alarming to me. I began to question if we, as a society, were failing our young mothers. Were we holding them accountable to being good mothers, but not holding them accountable to finding out who they were as individuals? Were we not empowering them to stay connected to their dreams, even after having a child? Were we equipping these young mothers to pursue a life of success, or pushing them into a life of poverty?

As I continued in my speaking career, my audience expanded to adult mothers. I would often share my experiences and speak to them about walking in their purpose and pursuing their dreams. Soon I began to find myself engaged in conversations with adult women that were surprisingly similar to the conversations I had with teen mothers. These women knew they were put on this earth to do something great, but felt "stuck" and didn't know how to identify what it was they were called to do. Others would speak of the dreams they once had for themselves that had gone unfulfilled for one reason or another, and expressed a desire to reconnect with them.

Interacting with both groups of mothers gave me a sobering reality of the state that a lot of mothers were in. It was after these experiences that I realized that more voices like mine needed to be heard. These moms need to see and hear from others who could relate to their experiences and give them hope by showing them that success for them is still possible, even when their situations make it hard to believe. They need to know that in spite of the abuse, rejection, shame, multiple pregnancies, responsibilities, and whatever else they may have going on, they still have a purpose in this world.

In a society where teen motherhood is still a taboo topic and young mothers are automatically labeled as failures, my hope is that this book will break the stereotype and be an example of hope and inspiration for you. In a society where mothers are made to feel ashamed to go after what THEY want, I want this book to be proof that you can unapologetically pursue your dreams and still be good mothers, wives, friends, etc.

Most importantly, I want this book to cause you to TAKE ACTION. List one goal that will make the biggest change in your life and begin doing one or two actions EACH DAY to accomplish that goal.

Remember how I told you that because my life as a young single mother was not as I expected it to be, I devalued myself and my capabilities and thus, made a lot of poor decisions and limited my success? Well, I overcame that and began experiencing major breakthroughs in my life because I changed my mindset, realized my self-worth, and learned to believe in the possibility of my dreams. YOU can have this too. You can accomplish your goals, step by step, by taking daily action.

You are worth it! Your dreams and destiny are your

birthright. You deserve all the good things that the moms in this book have and you can do the work it takes to achieve your goals. Life is filled with challenges and hard work – whether or not you pursue your destiny. Since you are already faced with tremendous challenges, why not take on the ones that will give you and your family the best rewards instead of focusing on the ones with little benefit? All it takes is a bit of redirection, refocus, a plan, determination, and effort. And you can do this! If we could accomplish the things we did, so can you. Today is the day when you step into your new life. Today is the day when you will start your journey to become the woman you were meant to be. Today is your day. And you are ready!

So, to answer the question regarding who is a Millionaire M.O.M...YOU are a Millionaire M.O.M.!

Unleash Your Fortune

You birthed a baby, but can you birth your dreams? We, as mothers, tend to be natural nurturers; we nurture our children, our families, our friends...the list goes on and on. We endure the battle scars of the experiences of broken relationships, rejection, abuse, and still somehow manage to happily come to the aid of others. However, the one thing we most often overlook nurturing is ourselves. We sense that we are called to do something great in this world and we envision ourselves living those dreams full out but those dreams quickly take a back seat to whatever our life demands at the moment. By the time we finally take the time to revisit the greatness inside of us, we no longer recognize it. It's been so long since we've envisioned it that we've even forgotten what it looks like.

In some cases, we've gone through so much throughout our lives that we never realized its existence. Once we begin to be reminded of our dreams, we question our value and ability to bring it to fruition because it is now buried underneath years of negative experiences and thoughts – hurt, regret, feeling less than or not good enough, as well as the shame and rejection from having children at a young age and out of wedlock. How can we reach our greatness with all of this "stuff" in the way? Is it even worth digging through all of that "stuff" to get to it? How one chooses to answer these questions is what separates those that achieve success from the ones who live a stagnant life and never realize just how great they really are.

Sorting Through the "Stuff"

The fact of the matter is, in order to reach the greatness that is inside of you and unleash your fortune, you must first sort through the "stuff" that is keeping it buried. My greatness was buried under an unforgiving spirit. It was not that I couldn't forgive someone else, but it was myself that I could not forgive. Being unforgiving caused me to devalue, and even at times, sabotage my own dreams, resulting in me only achieving limited success in various areas of my life. It was only after I got to the root of my need to be unforgiving and identified the things that I was holding against myself, which I discuss later in my chapter, that I was truly able to face my truths, forgive myself, and move forward.

For a lot of us, sorting through our "stuff" can be a daunting and undesirable task, simply because some of those things we'd rather not revisit. However, it is very necessary because, while we may find that some of the "stuff" we come across is no longer needed or valid, some of the things we uncover may be items that can be repurposed and utilized for good.

Embracing the Process

The process of sorting through the "stuff," or decluttering, is a lifelong commitment. Initially, it may seem overwhelming because there may be a lot of clutter to sort through – past hurts, negative experiences, limiting beliefs, and other issues. However, as you begin to clear out that clutter, you will shift into more of a "maintenance" mode. That's because once you've gone through and decluttered most of the "stuff," you will be able to more quickly identify things that are worth keeping in your space and you will have less of a desire to allow clutter back in.

Listed below are the steps that should be taken when you begin your journey of decluttering and unleashing your fortune:

1. **Identify the "stuff."** In order to be able to identify the clutter in your life, you must become self-aware. This can be accomplished first through prayer and meditation. Give yourself at least fifteen minutes a

day of silence to really hear your soul speak to you. Reflect on your actions, interactions, reactions, and thoughts throughout the day. Ask yourself why you acted, reacted, interacted, or thought the way you did that day, and be transparent and honest with yourself about those reasons. What is the "stuff?" Why is it there? What other "stuff" is associated with it? This revelation may not happen in one day. It may take a few days or more of prayer and reflection to really be able to identify the "stuff" that is cluttering your life and your fortune.

2. **Assess its value.** Once you have identified the "stuff" in your life, you must then assess its value. Is this "stuff" helping you to move forward in your life or thrusting you backward? Is it keeping you stuck? How does this "stuff" make you feel? Is it valid? Is it needed?

3. **Put it in its proper place.** After determining the validity and necessity of the "stuff" you have identified, you must put it in its proper place. Too often we allow things a front row or driver's seat in our lives when they only deserve a balcony view or no view at all. Is the "stuff" you've identified worth keeping, or should it be discarded? If it is something that you

wish to keep, are you willing to put it in its proper place? If it is something that needs to be discarded, are you ready to let go of it? In some cases, letting go may require forgiveness – forgiveness of others who are attached to the "stuff," or maybe even yourself.

Affirming Yourself

"It's the repetition of affirmations that leads to belief. And once that belief becomes a deep conviction, things begin to happen."

-Muhammad Ali

Bad habits are hard to break. The same applies to negative thoughts and actions. Now that you've gotten rid of the negative "stuff" that was cluttering your life, you must quickly replace it with positive things. It is critical for you to rewire those years of negative thoughts and actions. Even in the Bible, the importance of positive affirmation is mentioned, "From the fruit of their mouth a person's stomach is filled; with the harvest of their lips they are satisfied. The tongue has the power of life and death, and those who love it will eat its fruit," Proverbs 18:20-21.

The coming stories are divided into five sections, with each section introducing a key affirmation, followed by a Millionaire M.O.M. challenge to help you embrace your inner Millionaire M.O.M. Get ready to unleash your fortune!

I. I Am Greater Than My Circumstances

"The most common way people give up their power is by thinking they don't have any."

— *Alice Walker*

I no longer allow my circumstances to dictate my future. I am creating a life that goes beyond the limitations of my surroundings. I define my new normal and raise the bar of expectation for my life. I refuse to live a life of mediocrity, and I know and believe that things can and will get better because I am in complete control and have God on my side.

Chandra Pointer: Pregnant with Purpose

Motherhood can be a challenging journey for even the most equipped and experienced mom. Having a child and being able to be the best mother possible to your child (who depends on you for everything: food, shelter, water, love, and guidance), proves to be rewarding and enlightening. It can also prove to be the most difficult and challenging role a woman can have; especially a teen girl.

Now picture this...

A 15-year-old adolescent girl who is an honor student, very active at school, and well liked. She has a large family that is plagued with multiple dysfunctions. Mom is a single parent on public assistance with minimal education. Dad pays child support, barely visits and is a functioning alcoholic. There is one example of a loving relationship in her family. Two, maybe three, college graduates, and one entrepreneur. No one owns anything. Poverty is her last name; first name, "Generational." She lives in a drug and crime infested, low-income housing project. Teen pregnancy is the norm. In fact, it seems accepted and celebrated. She is now the mother of a tiny human being whom she has to nurture, raise, love, feed, hug; all the things she currently needs. Some of these things, she doesn't know how to do. But she is eager to show the world how to be a real parent. She promises herself and her unborn child she will be the best parent she can be. Yet she doesn't understand the challenges of being a parent. So she fails at it for a long, long time.

Hi, Mom-on-a-Mission!

My name is Chandra Pointer. I am a wife, mother, mentor, entrepreneur and I was that teen mom. I know some of the challenges you have or might be experiencing. And I can assure you it is not the end of the world. In fact, it can be the beginning of a journey that will change your life for the better.

In this chapter, I will share with you my story, my challenges, and how I overcame many obstacles as a teen mom. It is my hope that you identify with some things, allow those things to help you make wise decisions from this day forward, and know that being a teen mom is not the end of the road for you.

Here is my story and 12 Lessons I learned from being

a Teen Mom. On October 11, 1993, I went to sleep a pregnant teen and woke up the next day to become the mother of a beautiful baby girl. I can remember telling God on that day, "I don't know what I'm doing, but please help me be the best mother I can be."

How did I get there? I was 15-years-old, in junior high school, and pregnant. I was the only girl in my 9th-grade class with a little person growing inside of her. Clueless and ashamed, I felt daily as I tried to hide the fact that I would be a mother soon. At the time, I didn't even know what being a mother meant. What do mothers do with and for their children? What do they say to their children? After all, I was just a child myself who still needed her mom. I didn't know what to do with a crying or sick baby. I didn't know where to look for help or what questions to ask. So I began mimicking the actions of a woman who was my mom but was failing at being a mother.

Lesson One

You are your children's first role model. They will mimic everything they see you do. Strive to set a great example.

My mom was my grandmother's eighth child and

second daughter and she was loved by many. We had a lot of extended family members in the Foote Holmes Housing Projects where I was raised and lived until I moved away after marrying in 2003. Yes, I spent 25 years of my life in a drug and crime infested neighborhood where grown men prey on young girls and it was accepted. My mom, doing what she could, had absolutely no time to monitor me or my whereabouts. She was firm yet unbothered. She provided the essentials yet neglected to provide the love I needed. Therefore, she did not nurture me or our relationship and it became strained because I needed her more now that I was to be a mother and she couldn't step up.

Lesson Two

The well-being and safety of your children are your sole responsibility. Children who feel safe and cared for are most likely to avoid damaging situations and making foolish decisions.

The day that I found out I was pregnant, I told my mom I was keeping my baby. I was angry and made a point to let her know that I was now in control. I was angry because I needed her and wanted her attention and presence so badly. But no. She was practically living another life with her boyfriend on the other side of town – leaving me and my

20

siblings to fend for ourselves while she carried on like she'd never had us. I thought that my announcement would change her response to me or make her return home, but it didn't.

The anger I felt toward her consumed me as I chanted every day, "I don't want to be nothing like her," yet I still admired her and looked up to her. Even through the anger I felt toward her, she still remained my role model – someone I admired and wanted to be like. She was a hardworking hairstylist who lacked the education and knowledge that could have been her ticket out of the ghetto for a new life and a new environment for her children.

My childhood was rough but I also experienced some of the best days of my life. I can remember having everything I needed and even though I lived in the "hood," you couldn't tell me we didn't have the best life materialistically. My mom, a single parent, sold drugs and did hair in our three-bedroom apartment to support us. Every day we had a house full of people. Some I knew, some I didn't. I just remember always feeling like it was too much. I never came home to a quiet house until she moved out to live with her boyfriend, taking my four-year-old sister with her. I was fifteen years old at the time.

With this new independence and a whole lot of anger, I entered junior high school with my self-esteem in the dumps and looking for anyone who could validate me no matter what I had to sacrifice. My mother never talked to me about sex, pregnancy, or diseases. The streets and my friends were my sources of information and most of the time their information was wrong or too late. As a result, I contracted a sexually transmitted disease the same day I lost my virginity to an 18-year-old to whom I lied and told I wasn't a virgin.

Lesson Three

Talk to your children often. Communication and spending time with your children can buffer outside sources of misinformation about sex, drugs, and pregnancy.

So, I had this beautiful baby girl who became my life. I made sure she had the best of everything I could give her. I got my first job at age 16 at a pizza parlor on Beale St., Memphis, Tennessee. I was so proud to be able to provide for myself and my child. She became my little best friend. It was all about me and her. I possessed no real parenting skills, so I did what I saw my mom do. My mom made sure I always had the latest fashion, that I had my hair combed, a nice, hot dinner. I had lacked for nothing but her love and presence. Even though, as I realized this to be true and became even more bitter, it was exactly what I started doing with my child.

But I was still determined to graduate and luckily for me, my high school had a daycare for children of teen moms. This enabled me to finish high school and graduate with my class on time. Feeling lonely and lacking support during this time was the start of my self-talks. I would tell myself all the time "Chandra, you have no excuse. If you don't graduate from high school, you deserve to stay right where you are." Often I would plead to God "Please God. This can't be my life. I just know this is not my future." To live in poverty, have babies, and expect that the government would help me take care of me and my child. No, that's not Chandra's future! I didn't quite know how I was going to change my situation. I sure didn't have the answer. Only disappointment, determination and discontent fueled my actions. $142 of monthly aid for a child and mother…Who can live on that? "This can't be it, GOD!" I would cry out when I was frustrated with my circumstances.

My self-talks kept me grounded in faith and helped

me gain clarity about what I wanted out of life and how to obtain it. Self-talking is a great tool to use to get you through some of life's most challenging obstacles because there will be times when there is no one around to push you, motivate you, or hold you accountable. You know what you need more than anyone. So speak life to yourself and encourage yourself daily.

Say it right now:

"I can do this.

"I must do this."

"I going to do this."

Now, go and make IT happen M.O.M.!

Lesson Four

Education is your first tool to a better life. By all means, graduate high school. The feeling of accomplishment will take you a long way. It is the first domino to escaping poverty.

A lot was going on around me and inside of me as an adolescent. To escape from the conflict I was feeling, I engulfed myself in every school activity that I was capable of doing. I was an honor student, cheerleader, on the pom-pom squad, acted in plays, ran for the queen of this and queen of that, ran track, broadcast journalism, and more, to escape from my reality and I yearned for someone to be proud of me.

As I went through my high school years, I continued to struggle with low self-esteem. My friends seemed to think I had it all together. I was smart. My hair was always done and I wore the latest fashions. On the outside, I looked great but on the inside, the emotional conflict I was experiencing began to surface and affected me academically. I started cutting school, drinking, and smoking weed. The pressure of motherhood began to feel burdensome. I felt like I was missing out on having fun with my friends. I felt trapped. My child's father was doing what he wanted. He had his freedom and this made me angry and resentful. Out of frustration I left my child with my mom and uncle for them to raise. *How ironic and immature of me to abandon my child when I had experienced so much neglect and poor parenting in their care already?* My siblings and I saw too much too soon. I just didn't know any better and today I understand my mom and uncle didn't either.

In spite of my reckless behavior and dysfunctional environment, I graduated high school May 1996. Graduating from high school gave me the confidence I needed to keep going and fighting for my future. The feeling of accomplishment made me feel like I can do anything I set my mind to. There are so many things that I had to come up against living in the hood, but God! I know today HE had a purpose for my life then and now. HE specializes in finishing what he starts. HE knows what we need before we can even ask. He knew the desires of my heart and one of those desires was to be able to take care of my children without doing something illegal or placing them in harm's way.

Lesson Five

Don't be afraid to ask for help. There are so many resources available to you in your community. Ask a friend or a family member. Pick up the phone. It is ok not to know. It is not ok not to know and never ask.

As a fifteen-year-old mother, things are expected of you. People assume you know things when you are truly clueless. You lose friends because when you have to go home and take care of your child after school while they're headed to hang out and have fun. Your conversations are

26

about pacifiers and Pampers; theirs are about playing and partying.

Before I was working age, I obtained employment. Getting a job was not up for debate. After all, I had to take care of my child and keep up this image my mom created by looking like life was good when it was far from the truth. We lived way outside of our means and the only thing we had of value was each other. Though we were not picture perfect, my family and I enjoyed each other's company and created a lot of fun memories together that I cherish today.

Working gave me freedom, a sense of responsibility and security. I loved the fact that I did not have to ask anyone for anything, not even my child's father. The pride I felt in being responsible challenged me to do more. I had dreams of graduating and living on my own. So I quietly prepared to be on my own. I worked. I saved and moved into my first apartment at age nineteen.

My cousin Velma imparted in me work ethic and integrity. She was dedicated to her job, but she was more dedicated to the future of her son. She was the big sister I wanted and didn't have. I admired her strength as a single mom. She was my resource center. A place where I could go to get all the information I needed and to ask all the questions I could think of without judgment. From relationships to living on my own, she was always ready and willing to share all she had with me. I am forever grateful for her presence in my life.

Lesson Six

> *Working a job can boost your self-confidence and public assistance will handicap you. Living on your own allows you to control the environment in which your child lives, learns, and grows so strive for independence.*

Living on my own had its perks. The only drawback was that I moved out of one hood and into another. Same kind of people, same daily activities, same mentality – just a different location. I was proud of the strides I was making despite the loneliness I felt. My new place provided the peace I needed to start turning my life around, but first I wanted to play house and have fun.

Still unaware of who I was, I entered relationship after relationship. I invited all the chaos in my life by living it literally through my vagina. There was a time I thought that giving my soul to a man guaranteed he would stay in my life.

28

Every three to six months, I would start the cycle again. Mentally depleted and frustrated from failed relationships, I no longer recognized myself. I had forgotten that I was the mother of a four-year-old little girl who needed me just like I needed my mom. Out of touch with my reality, I found it hard to be a mom when I needed and desired someone to love, hug, validate, affirm, and encourage me too.

Having my own place to live and raise my children and the income to support us made life much easier. When I didn't agree with situations and the behavior of people, I felt blessed to have a home to retreat to and get away from it all and to protect my children (yes, at this point I had my second daughter) from outside influences. My independence allowed my children the freedom to be just children and this made me the happiest.

Lesson Seven

You subliminally and unconsciously teach your children about love, communication, and relationships.

Real relationships for me were far and few between. My relationship with my mother suffered. My best friend and I stopped all communication without clarity or warning,

29

and the only real love I felt was from my aunt Joann. Every time I was in her presence, she made sure I knew how smart and beautiful I was. Those seeds of affirmation that she planted carried me into young adulthood. Her example made me want to strive for a better life.

On the other hand, the loneliness I felt was overwhelming. I was getting tired of dating with no purpose. Soul dying and emotionally frustrated, I searched for fulfillment in a relationship with the one who knew me better than anyone: my creator. I started going to church and reading my Bible even though I remained on the fence of life. I didn't want to change initially. But at this point, I didn't have a choice. I felt safe in my situation and disgusted by it at the same time. My relationship with God gave me a sense of calm. I now wanted what God wanted for me and everything I did from this stage of my life onward was to prevent my children from experiencing unnecessary hurt and wallowing in the struggles of life. It took so many years to get focused and get my mind right. I had a vague plan in my head to get away from it all, I just didn't know where to start and definitely couldn't envision my future. All I knew for sure was that I was going to embrace every opportunity presented to me and stay positive, optimistic, and keep it moving even if it killed me.

Frustrated with fast food restaurants, low wages, and telling the Department of Human Services all my business, I decided to go to school and obtain a skill. When you have children, your attitude about life, work, and relationships has to change for the betterment of your future.

You must make sacrifices if you want to see a change in your life. Breaking generational curses starts with you being tired of the "Mama did it, so-it-must-be-right-disease." What worked for your family may not work for you and your children. I simply did not want to raise my children in the hood. I wanted them to have the opportunity to grow up in an environment that nurtured and promoted their growth and development. I didn't care who agreed or not. I was willing to lose all I knew to ensure that my children would have a chance at a better life.

While in a very toxic relationship with my second daughter's father, I found the gumption in me to go to school and prove to him that I didn't need him. I didn't know at the time that shutting him down, shutting him out, wasn't going to change my situation one bit. I began to realize that people only change when it hurts too bad to remain the same and I was beyond tired and drowning in anger. So, I started nursing school in 2000 in an attempt to get my life on track. I now had some clarity about the direction I was headed and the world opened up to me and changed my perspective. It wasn't easy, though.

I experienced every setback imaginable in school. No transportation to clinical, two medication errors during clinical, two fights on campus, no babysitter for my kids, no family support, and the ultimate: failing a class before finals and missing one question that almost stopped me from graduating.

But I was determined to let NOthing or NO person stop me from becoming a nurse. I became Chandra Wright, Licensed Practical Nurse, May 12, 2000, with a 1-year-old on one hip and a 7-year-old holding my hand. I did it! I did it for my children…I did it for me!

Even though I was making great strides in my life, I still struggled emotionally to keep it all together. I had those days when I didn't feel like I deserved to be happy or successful. I cried a lot as a young adult. Not from sadness but from being sick and tired of the battle to not be the girl who would give up or give in. If I didn't do anything else with my life at this point, I taught my children that with faith and hard work they could do and be anything they put their minds to. My soul was at peace but it wasn't satisfied, so I challenged myself to climb yet another mountain – having a loving and healthy relationship.

Lesson Eight

> *Insanity is doing the same thing and expecting a different result. Change your mindset. Change your life!*

A loving relationship for a single mom with two children, I was convinced did not exist. Most young women I knew were raising their child or children by themselves. Motherhood does something to the psyche of a teenage girl. Having a baby before you are equipped and ready can be stressful, especially if there are no guidance or loving relationships available to carry you through those days when you want to succumb to the pressure and demands of motherhood. You now work 24/7 with no days off.

Take it from me, *I want to raise my kids as a single mother,* said no woman ever. No mother wants to raise her children alone. I wanted different for my children. I got past the wishful thinking and prepared myself to date with a purpose. I was determined to date with my future in mind.

I stopped dating and shacking up to avoid loneliness. I started looking at my current situation from my daughters' perspectives. I became aware that they were watching me. How dare I enforce expectations on them when I wasn't practicing what I preached? It mattered to me what they thought about me. I wanted to teach them how to date and how to carry themselves. To be the person they would desire to marry one day. After all, who else would teach them with their best interest in mind?

I decided to give myself a break after being in a very physically and emotionally abusive relationship. I wanted to experience how it felt to be alone. Freedom from expectations. Freedom from the maintenance of a relationship. To hear myself think. To figure out what I really wanted. Most of all, to find the love within. That was a challenge because I thought loving yourself was being selfish.

A year later I was ready to start dating again, but this time, it was going to be different. I now loved me and I had boundaries. For the first time I wasn't afraid to be alone and wait until I found someone ready and worthy. No more children out of wedlock. No more shacking up or playing house. I was changing the path of my daughters' future. First, I had to believe I was worthy of the love I desired. Most importantly, I was breaking generational curses off my children and their children. I understood what that meant and every decision I made was based on that fact.

Lesson Nine

Love starts with you and flows to your children. Unhealthy relationships rob children of loving nurturing parents. Loving your children starts with making good choices and decisions.

I met my husband and best friend on the job at age twenty-three. My mind was made up that he was not *my type* and that he was *too nice*. We all know that *he's-too-good-to-be-true* syndrome that makes us fearful of settling down. Low self-esteem and self-sabotage can easily have you thinking you are not worthy to be loved because you have children.

He was a gentleman, a kind of man I had never encountered before. He wanted to date me, get to know my children, and help me follow my dreams. I was not used to a man knowing what he wanted and I was shocked that he wanted it with me. I couldn't understand why he wanted a woman with kids and I was sure he would leave me when he got what he wanted. So I thought. Silly me.

Ray and I married in November 2004. I took a leap of faith and uprooted my children to move to Chicago and give them the life they deserved. The best of both worlds: a mother and a father raising and loving them together.

Marriage was complicated for me. I was guarded, selfish, and did not trust easily. The smallest problems would cause me to throw my hands up. I considered divorce so much in the first year that I was sure my husband would walk away. But he stayed and endured. The sacrifices he made and the verbal abuse he experienced due to my unresolved anger issues, was evidence that he was a real man – one who doesn't walk away because things are rough at the moment. Allowing myself to be loved and feel love was new to me. So much so that I wasn't aware I wasn't loving and nurturing to my own children. I mean I fed them, dressed them, provided for them but it I wasn't nurturing them. I didn't know how.

I now had a family and structure. This situation was

new to my children. They weren't used to having parents and structure. My oldest daughter rejected our new life and as we settled into our new world, the effects of being a single teen parent with generational curses surfaced and threatened to destroy the legacy we were attempting to build for our children.

They say history repeats itself and if you don't master something you are bound to repeat it. In my struggle to grow in every area of my life, especially in being a mother, I discovered I was broken and angry and needed someone to teach me how to love and communicate with my daughters before they grew up feeling like I felt as a teen: angry, bitter, and confused.

Lesson Ten

*You cannot give your children something you
do not possess. You have to love and be loving in
order to give it away.*

It was all too much for my oldest daughter. She learned that the father she knew and lovingly called daddy, was not her dad. It was a big blow to the entire family. I had to pick myself up and keep going. I also found out she had been molested repeatedly by family members and friends.

Devastated and numb from the heartbreaking news, I didn't know how to help her. My husband and I exhausted every avenue to help my daughter get through all that she was feeling. The helplessness and pain you feel when you want to help your child cope and move through her struggles but can't, feels like a really bad sore throat. No matter what you do, it remains.

Lesson Eleven

Please do not allow different people to babysit your children. They are safer in a childcare facility with trained staff that is being monitored. Children become sexual prey when they have different and frequent caregivers.

I fell into a deep depression trying to save my daughter. She was broken. She ran away a lot to escape the pain she felt. I felt hopeless as a parent. Everyone who knew our situation tried to help us. Our attempts were unsuccessful as she continued to spiral out of control. My daughter taught me a lot about listening and communicating. She also taught me that teen girls are strong and need to express their feelings in a way that's comfortable for them and that it differs from girl to girl. The helplessness I felt placed me in the shoes of all mothers who struggle to develop and maintain a healthy relationship with their daughters.

As a result of our strained relationship, on April 26, 2013, I kicked off a mentoring program called SisterNation Inc. in Harvey, Illinois. The services SisterNation Inc. provides were born out of the lifelong passion and zeal to **support** young women as they develop and transition through adolescence. SisterNation Inc. provides opportunities for young women to achieve self-discovery by the following: relinquishing past personal challenges in one-on-one and group settings, modeling **sisterhood** by providing support to peers, and developing relevant **service** projects that address community needs. Sisterhood. Support. Service.

I had made it over the hump of depression and God was calling me to mentor young women and give them a platform to be heard and loved without judgment. I didn't think I could do it because my relationship with my daughter still suffered. But the need for the program was burning a hole in my soul. It became my therapy. Just when I thought I was there to teach the young ladies something, they ended up teaching me. I don't want any girl to experience what I went through as a teen. The pain of guilt, shame, low self-esteem and depression is real and it will hold your beautiful life hostage.

I truly believe if early on I would have had someone to talk to, to hug me, to affirm me, to say *I love you, you are beautiful, you are smart, you are going to be somebody one day*, I would have escaped some things because I would have known I deserved better and "learning and knowing you deserve better" takes time.

Lesson Twelve

There are no books on perfect parenting. All mothers learn as they go. Be open to learning from your children. Do your best and God will do the rest! Being a mother is the greatest blessing.

M.O.M., allow yourself to forgive, heal, love, and grow through all the obstacles you must and will face. I hope you are empowered and inspired to keep your head up in spite of current circumstances and situations. You're reading others' stories and testimonies and discovering that you are not in this alone and being a teen mom is not the end of the world for you. These stories can give you hope when you are feeling hopeless, strength when you are feeling tired, and peace when motherhood seems chaotic. There will be more good days than bad – trust me.

Motherhood is the beginning of a better version of you with the little people who love you UNCONDITIONALLY, watching! Take care and keep moving forward M.O.M.!

Corita Key: How Did I Get Here?

How Did I Get Here?

How did I get here? That's the big question. A damn-near 30-year-old woman stuck at her mother's home raising five small kids. If you had asked me thirteen years ago where I thought my life going, it definitely wouldn't be the life I'm currently living out. What would possess such a talented young woman to go down a path so clearly full of obstacles, you ask? I know, you're thinking it had to have been the result of one of the many stereotypes: a single parent home, peer pressure, low self-esteem or pure ignorance. Wrong! Well actually in my particular case, you're sort-of right. Many of these issues did play a major role in my current situation. Though, if it were not for my current situation and learning from my past mistakes, I would not be able to fulfill my mission in life. My mission is to help advance youth, families, and communities in any way possible. I invite you in on my journey from teen mom to millionaire mom. Let's start at the beginning. Are you ready?

Ready or Not!

"Ready or not, here you go!" This is a phrase many

pregnant young girls become all too familiar with once they become teen moms. There are no number of parenting classes or baby workshops that can prepare anyone, especially a teen, for the responsibilities ahead. My experience as a teen mom came at the tender age of seventeen. I was in my junior year when I got caught up in a relationship that ended in my getting pregnant.

Like most teen girls in high school, I believed having boyfriends and being in intense relationships was the thing to do at a young age. Yes, I had great academic achievements and I was very social. I was on just about every school team that existed. However, nothing – not even my drive for being involved – could deter me from the challenging course of teen parenting.

I never thought, like perhaps the women before me, that this would happen to me. I was the teen who could have learned a lot from other people's mistakes. But, none of the motivational speeches, life lessons, and bold warnings against getting pregnant too early would prove to be a deterrent for a self-absorbed teen who knew it all.

The year before I became pregnant, I remember making nasty, judgmental comments about peers who had gotten pregnant. I remember thinking, *that's what they get! I'm glad that's not me.* On the other hand, I would ask myself how they managed so well. I realize now the false sense of reality I perceived as they wobbled around like everything was just peachy keen was far from the truth. It was a complete façade and extreme naïveté on my part. It seemed as though motherhood was so easy and accepted. They wore the most fashionable maternity clothes, conducted bring your baby to school days (as if it was show and tell) and bragged about how they got to pass the baby off on granny and lived stress-free lives.

I was also influenced at a young age by the perfect picture painted by my wonderful mother. She had given me one of the best childhoods anyone could ask for: A childhood filled with a youthful, fun, patient, and loving mother. I believed that parenthood had to be easy – planned or not. And secretly, I admired that life. Unfortunately, this very attitude and jaded perception got me in trouble because, although I had the best mother ever, my childhood was not free of traumatizing events. Growing up with young parents definitely had its drawbacks.

Then, my brother died and I experienced extreme

grief. It also sparked an anger in me that was so out of control that not even the religion my dear mother and grandmother spoke of so frequently could comfort me. As I grew older, the television became my best friend. I went from the subliminal exposure of misogynistic and sexualized "kid" shows to explicit and exponential negative exposure when I discovered video channels. I admired video girls, taking in everything I saw. The hypnotizing lyrics from the negative music played in my mind as I imitated what I watched. Once I made friends and started going out, the damning reality of the events and the unrealistic perceptions that made up my life produced a dynamic problem and, even more, a damaged young girl.

Pregnancy Pains

But let me get back to my pregnancy, which was horrible. It caused me to leave high school early because I developed hyperemesis, a condition that makes have severe morning sickness throughout the entire day for the whole nine months. This was my first taste of the reality of pregnancy. It was not at all what it seemed. Well, at least not for me, especially since I became extremely ill and sickly looking and I trudged around school with an actual cup of spit, another side effect of my pregnancy. But, many people did not get to see this side of me. Like I stated before, I was a knock-out student both academically and socially, which led to my early graduation. So, you can imagine my surprise when my peers and teachers started treating me differently, as if this was the first time they'd seen a pregnant teen. Maybe they just couldn't accept this development from me.

At first, I hid my pregnancy. However, my parents knew better. Both my mother and grandmother, who had just gone on the "no pregnancy rants" two months earlier, had a sense about the situation. It didn't help that my so called boyfriend did not support me. I felt so alone. I had one supportive friend who helped me all the way through this very tough situation. Not only did I endure stigmatization and stereotyping from my peers and the faculty of the school, but I had to bear the entire situation all over again once the word got out at home. I learned what it meant to stand up for yourself after the scandal broke out in my family. Not only was I the target of disappointing looks and harsh, "I told you so's," so was my mother. I looked on as she defended herself when she was blamed for my bad decisions. Although mine was a difficult circumstance to accept, she defended me like a mother lion defending her cub. I was ridiculed by family members, physicians, case workers, and nosey strangers from this point on.

We Deserve Decency Too

One of the things I went through during my pregnancy that was most unpleasant was the search for a primary care provider and clinic that didn't make me feel *less than* for being a pregnant teen – as though my voice and my concerns didn't matter because I was young. In 2004, teen pregnancy was not uncommon, but some clinics were more accepting of and helpful to young clients. The problem for me was the travel because these clinics were far into the city. I can't stress the importance of having a primary care doctor who cares for you and with whom you have a great rapport. Going through a new and scary situation such as carrying and giving birth to another human being really requires a good medical relationship with a doctor and clinic. I was really disappointed when it was time to deliver my first child because my physician was on vacation and wasn't there for me. I was stuck in the hospital with over a half a dozen physicians and aids peering between my legs. I didn't think it took that many people to deliver one baby, and I was left feeling violated and like a guinea pig. I made sure that didn't happen the next three times because I learned how to advocate for myself and do my research.

Advocating for myself was a hard skill to develop and I still struggle with it sometimes. It is very easy to let someone tell you what to do or to speak to you any way they want when you feel shame, fear, guilt, and are unsure about many of the things you're doing because it is your first time. It was very hard to learn to care for someone while I was so young. I didn't have good management skills or any knowledge of how to care for someone. I didn't realize how much time it would take – all day, every day. My being so carefree a person and so babied by my mother was not a good history to have for this lifelong job.

Lesson Learned Too Late

After having my beautiful baby I learned two lessons: One, pick your partner wisely, and two, parenting is different for everybody. During my baby shower, I remember overhearing someone ask my partner what he wanted to do with his life after high school. The response he gave was shocking and downright embarrassing for me. He told my friends and family that he aspired to be rapper! Not an engineer, not a doctor. He had what I called, Rapper Syndrome,

Type 2. The deadly kind of self-centered, off track, in-the-streets mentality that wreaks havoc on families and relationships...very unhealthy. All I could do was pretend like I didn't hear his response as I looked away. The disturbing part was that while I had repeated a cycle, I had done it full circle: choosing a guy that would put me through the same troubles with the "rap life" that devastated my parents' relationship. A horrible occurrence like this happened again after having my second child, a boy who developed health-related issues passed down from his father. Such pertinent information is something one acquires in a working and mature relationship – a lesson I learned a little too late.

That's why it is very important to know your partner, his history, his goals, and aspirations. Once you have a baby with someone, you are in it together or, in some cases, alone. I can say I became just as disappointed once I learned I did not know myself either. I did not know what I wanted out of life or how to navigate in it after graduating from high school. I was a mess after my first child. The sleep deprivation and constant care-taking for someone else was not an easy transition for someone who was so sheltered and irresponsible. It did not help that my "Baby Blues" turned into full blown depression – undiagnosed of course, since I came from a family that had little interest in counseling and I was afraid to get help. And, having repeated the cycle, the pressure on me to be a strong, single mother like the generations before me, was unbearable. I felt like something was wrong, like I was less of a mother because I couldn't manage like the ones before me. I felt like it really put a distance between me and everybody in my life because I felt like they didn't understand. Which most of them didn't. They just expected me to move along and go with it. After all, I had done this to myself.

Straighten Out Your Issues

So, on top of the childhood issues, I developed illness on top of illness going through life without any type of treatment besides telling all my business to my mother, which also had its drawbacks. If I had known better, I would have advocated for myself. I would not have accepted the stereotypes that women were supposed to be super-women and even worse, super-natural mothers who shouldn't complain and know how to handle everything. This was another lesson I wish I had not had to learn. Years of despair not only took a toll on me, but my kids paid a big price, as did my family. All of this, coupled with a really unstable relationship, left two of my children emotionally scarred. My children experienced extreme emotional turmoil: grief, anger, and resentment from the age of six or less. I felt really bad as a parent and had no clue as to what to do. I just figured it would pass. I felt that the children would see that they weren't so different, since most families now-a-days are anything but traditional. Just as I left myself untreated and a mess, my kids became spitting images of me. If I could go back and change this I would give anything to do so.

I was in school all this time, just taking random classes. I ended up spending so much time at a two-year college that I may have well received my master's degree after graduating. It is really important to have goals, talk to advisors, get a mentor, and have a plan in place. Not knowing what to do or where to go is such a waste of precious time. I knew that I wanted to help people from a very early age. But the way I wanted to help people involved the arts at that time. I was afraid to leave that discipline to follow the career my mother had suggested after I'd had two kids: health care. I knew she was right, but I was reluctant. I felt health care was just not for me.

Along with the depression that made parenting hard,

I developed a two-fold resentment towards the kids which was extremely unhealthy. The first was due to their behavior towards me because of my complicated relationship with their father. He, who was not doing shit, seemed to have all the love, fun, and happy attitudes from them while I was treated with bad attitudes, complaints, confusion, and stress. I was working so hard for them. I also resented the fact that my mother kept telling me to put my dreams to the side for sake of someone else, ungrateful little someones at that. I felt worse as I realized the sacrifices my mother had to make. Learning that this was the way it would have to be from this point forth, giving up everything for the sake of my children, I questioned motherhood. I wasn't ready to give up everything. Was I a good mother? How could I be so selfish? It was too much. As a result, I became detached from my parental duties.

My family grew angry at me; so much so, they barely wanted to be around me. In the midst of all this, my kids' father and I were still involved. The routine seemed to repeat itself: happy for a little while, arguing and breaking up, make-up then pregnant, back to break-up again. So, I was on my third child in 2009. Two weeks before nursing school, I was ready, complete with a book bag full of resentment, anger, baby blues, and uncertainty about my viability as a student at the four-year university. I was in culture shock. The lack of support from my kids' father, and the array of home issues from the people who did support me affected my success. I ended up failing. My despair spiraled into a different type of low for almost two years. I learned an important lesson from this experience: Never let failure keep you down. I sat on my couch for close to three years wallowing in failure, unable to pick myself back up. I could not see the big picture telling me how the failure was a signal. Obviously, at that time in my life I was so consumed with personal grief and other issues that helping other people in life or death situations was extremely challenging.

Stepping Back and Making Changes

Not being in school, I had time to work through my anger and other issues. It helped that the third child with whom I'd barely had time to spend during the year of nursing school was such a lovely, easy going child, not affected by daddy issues like the other children. We got along pretty well and our bond helped change my mindset. I was able to put all my energy into making my kids feel happy and cared for. Back when I was in school, I would leave home for hours and hours to work or go to class then come home to study. That left me feeling extremely guilty. When I left school I was able to get back into the groove of teaching my kids new academic and social skills. It was simply living in the moment with them and I became involved in their school.

After realizing how I had made it hard for them at home, I worked on my attitude to change that atmosphere. I thought, *how could I not realize they were just kids? My kids.* They didn't ask to be brought into a stressful, poverty-stricken life by a selfish, immature mother who didn't know how to plan. But we worked on love and fell in love all over again. I felt like a mother again, and although I probably wasn't the best, at least we had a stronger bond. If I could not give them the finer things in life because of my economic status due to not having finished school yet, at least I could give them the type of childhood my mother gave me. I could give them a childhood filled with unconditional love, where a child would be unaware of the condition of his or her surroundings or be blind to the hardship mommy was going through because she put her children first, had the strength of God, and nurtured the love that withstood all madness.

Parent Involvement Matters

After really getting in tune with my kids, I noticed every little thing about them. I knew everything that made them happy or bothered them before they would open their mouths. Soon I noticed that my kids were suffering from something at school. This was unacceptable. My kids would come home in tears telling me how the teachers spent all day yelling and punishing the class due to behavioral issues, and how afraid they were of accidentally getting hurt by classmates who acted out in class with violent behavior. I reached out to faculty several times before I just became sick and tired of it all. It was hard to get my kids out of bed in the morning. The atmosphere was not conducive to learning. But after realizing my children were excelling academically almost to the point where they were not being challenged in the classroom, I said to myself *this is it*.

I spent the next couple of years fretting about how to get my children out of our school system. I began to research and become aware of how things were arranged outside of my safety net and I realized I could not afford to move or put the kids in private school. Even if I had found a job, the way the renting system was set up in the well-to-do towns seemed to ensure that anyone who did not belong there, stayed out. Not being able to break out of poverty and stress made me feel desperate and hopeless. There had to be another way. Depression began to creep in again as I searched for work day after day with no luck for almost two years.

A New Chapter

I began undergraduate studies in social work. My studies helped me to define advocacy and activism, which was at the very core of what I was doing before almost giving up. I excelled in class and my professors were amazing. They sparked a new attitude in me that made me believe I could do anything while empowering me with the tools to do it. That definitely gave me confidence. Instead of complaining and feeling hopeless, I began to get involved in the school system again. Changing my attitude and my environment was at the top of my list of priorities. I began to get recognition from the teachers and faculty. Before, I'd had just a brief interaction with them consisting of them telling me how my children were amazing and different from most of the children. Then we began to actually build relationships and listen to each other.

Instead of complaining to the teachers and faculty, I

began to think of ways to create change. Since the teachers didn't change when I had first complained, I figured maybe they would respond differently if I had a plan in place. I learned that when teachers and faculty members see that you are involved, they respond to that family differently. But, I couldn't bear other kids falling between the cracks. I began patrolling the school to watch out for my kids and make sure they had less stressful days. Then I developed an affinity for all the children regardless of their behavior. One night I realized I was meant to stay there to make a difference!

However, things didn't go smoothly from this point at all. I realized it was going to take a much bigger investment of time and support to the schools to make even the slightest difference. There were so many rules in place, very minimal support from the very busy parents, and board members who made all of the decisions due mainly to the absence of any parent input. This left more obstacles to work through. On top of that, in 2014 during my junior year of undergrad studies, I had gotten pregnant again. This time with twins.

My support to the school came to a halt as I became

ill again and had to leave school for a while. I was devastated. I couldn't believe I'd let this happen again. And again, the same routine carried itself out as my kids' father and I had broken up. But I couldn't stop moving. I continued with school as soon as I became stable. Though my leave of absence had caused me to receive an incomplete grade, I was actually able to get an A out of the class! This was all the motivation I needed. The following semester I was present for classes, sick or not. I stayed on top of my work and received so much support from my teachers and peers. They really commended me on staying in school even though I could have gone into labor any minute. Of course, my beautiful living angel of a mother was there, supporting me every step of the way. She told me that I could do this! We talked about my chances of getting postpartum depression after having the babies and what we were going to do from this point forward. We were basically back at square one again. But did she judge me? No! Did my peers judge me? No! I did, however, beat myself up badly. All of my plans were going to change again. My mother was still caring for me – a grown woman – and my, now, *five* kids. My mother worked two jobs to do this, and she did this with grace, strength, and devotion. I wanted to work but she only wanted me to stay in school. She believed in me so deeply and wanted me to focus only on family and school. Working was to be the last case scenario.

Adjust and Keep Moving Forward

This life with my mother taking care of me was hard to accept. It was very hard for me to forgive myself for making the same mistake I had made over thirteen years ago. But, my mother's faith in me and my capabilities kept me going. I kept pushing forward, and after a traumatic delivery, returned back to class within three weeks postpartum. I felt like I was having an out of body experience. I know I wasn't present. I kept having nightmares and visions of the traumatic C-section. I was just glad that we all made it out alive! I did, however, realize something was off about one of my twins.

I brought it up in the hospital but got a general response. I didn't pursue the issue further because I figured it was a hospital, and with as many tests they were running on my babies they would surely know if something was off with one of them. But in the back of my mind, I sensed something wasn't right. I took my concern to my doctors at the babies' first postpartum check-up and they also told me everything seemed ok. Then a few days later, while in class one night, I received a distressing call from my mother. "One of your doctors just called hysterically demanding for you to take the baby to the hospital, now!"

Something *was* wrong! I slumped down onto the bench outside the classroom instantly filled with raging anger. Anger towards the doctors and most of all a guilt-filled rage towards myself. I knew it. How could I let this happen when I knew how to advocate for myself and my kids?

In the hospital with my baby for a week, and away from the other twin as well as my other children, I had to endure the painstaking experience of doctors and nurse after nurse examining and poking my child. For my part, I just sang to my baby and kept my brave hat on the whole time. What weighed heavily on my heart was the thought that my family and I were reliving the painful situation that resulted in the loss of my dear brother years ago. I was scared.

After being told about transplant options and the daunting news of the upcoming frequent check-up visits, we were released from the hospital. He had been diagnosed with a rare type liver problem and the doctors didn't know what to make of the situation. I had to go back to school with all of these issues. My friends were very supportive and concerned. They didn't know how I was pulling through these situations. It was all thanks to one of the best mothers in the world and a very supportive family.

I also ended up building a relationship with my kids' father because of this. I definitely needed more help with the twins, although I was reluctant to put my trust in someone who had proven to be so unreliable. However, I had very few options. With my mother working two jobs, my internship starting, and my passion to stay active in the community, I figured we were going to have to work something out for everyone's sake. I'm glad to say it all worked out. There were a few bumps in the road, but we now communicate better than ever.

My mom always told me, "No matter what happens between you and him, together or not, you have to keep the kids in mind first."

We are definitely heeding that lesson. And we have yet to break-up. After a year of going back in forth to the hospital, I'm glad to report that the doctors cleared my son of having any health related issue. It resolved on its own!

Mothers Are Important

A year later in 2015, I heard of a scholarship opportunity, The Dr. Margaret T. Burroughs Scholarship Fund. After doing some research, I fell in love with Dr. Burroughs' work and her devotion to inspire people to be better and do better with history. I felt that we shared the same mission and values. I hesitated to apply for the scholarship. It was for mothers, but all my insecurities came rushing at me.

I thought maybe they would question why I had so many kids. Maybe they would think badly of me for placing such a heavy burden on my family. Maybe they would ask, "What the hell happened to the father?" and, "Why aren't you married after all of this?"

But, I kept coming back to the blank page on my computer screen. I felt so passionately about this and it involved the arts! Since art is where my heart had been since I was little, I went for it a couple of days before the deadline. I ran into so many obstacles trying to get all the documents needed to complete that application.

I couldn't get a simple transcript needed for reference. It took almost four hours to figure out how to get it from an outside source my school worked with and somehow they couldn't find me listed as a student! My printer at home wouldn't work and the computers at one of the libraries I would frequent were down. Time was running out and I was on the verge of giving up.

But I didn't give up and it made me confident since that was my first attempt at applying for a scholarship (now, I am less afraid and more optimistic about any application process). I won the scholarship and the award ceremony was held at the DuSable Museum of African American History. It was an experience I will never forget.

Here I am Today

I came to realize that my purpose on this earth is taking care of my kids and setting a good example for other stressed out mothers. I am passionate about helping young girls stay away from the hardship of teen parenthood as well as inspiring those who are facing this situation. As I am at the end of my studies, I am glad to say my reason for choosing a career in social work, to abate the stigma surrounding seeking help, hasn't changed!

As for my involvement in the community, I have

even gone beyond the school level into the political aspect of my community by attending school board and village meetings. I now know the level of difference that can be made by involvement, voting, and building relationships.

I have gained so much confidence, come out of my shell, and stopped the negative thinking about myself. I remember when I did my admissions interview for undergrad studies and my advisor asked me to tell her a little about myself. I said some basic things and ended with, "I'm just a mom." I will never forget how she stopped me in that moment and looked into my eyes and said, "Never say you are 'just' a mom. That job is hard work, and that's only half of who you are. Know your worth."

That is what this journey has helped me realize. My family and children mean more to me than anything in this world. All the things I do for them to better myself and better their lives, such as going to school, learning how to be more nurturing, and providing unconditional love no matter how hard times are, make me a Millionaire M.O.M.! Advocating and staying involved in the school and community to help my children and others is the icing on the cake! No television fantasy or media recognition can beat this life!

If you don't take anything away from my hardship, please consider this: Learn how to learn from other people's mistakes. Don't be afraid or ashamed to seek help. Forgive yourself, love yourself, and if you have children, think about the way you love them. Is it your best? Can you do better? Are you willing to learn or try? Never let failure, depression, fear or anything else steal years away from your precious life. With love,

M.O.M.

Millionaire *M.O.M.* Challenge #1

*"And the Lord answered me, and said, Write
the vision, and make it plain upon tables, that
he may run that readeth it."*

-The Holy Bible, Habakkuk 2:2

Having a vision for your life is important. However, it is even more important to write the vision down. Create a holistic vision board for your life. Include all areas of your life such as finances, career, family, relationships, health, spiritual, and whatever else you deem fit. Once completed, hang the board in a location where it will always be visible to you.

Reflect on the following questions:

1. What items on the board seem the easiest to achieve? Which seems more difficult?
2. What items are most important to you?
3. Are you willing to do what it takes to achieve the goals on your vision board?

67

II. I AM MORE THAN ENOUGH

"When I loved myself enough, I began leaving whatever wasn't healthy. This meant people, jobs, my own beliefs and habits – anything that kept me small. My judgment called it disloyal. Now I see it as self-loving."

— Kim McMillen

I am worth fighting for. I know that I have value to provide to the world and I am committed to unleashing my fortune for whomever I am called to. I educate and invest in myself on a regular basis. I know that inside of me I already have everything I need to succeed. I remove myself from toxic relationships and surround myself with positivity and people who push me to be greater.

Dorothea Cooper: Recover and Discover

My fondest memories of childhood are of music and my sisters, however growing up with older sisters is no walk in the park – especially when there is a huge age difference. I am the third of four girls and like most children with siblings, there is always a story to tell. My older sister would torture and harass me constantly. She would play mean tricks and give me the "I'm not your friend" silent treatment. Big deal right? Well, for me it was a big deal because I wanted nothing more than her love and acceptance. I even offered to pay her if she agreed to be my friend.

When my mother found out I was paying for my sister's friendship, I was in big trouble. My mother was strong and independent. The thought of me giving anything in order to get love and acceptance was frowned upon and I was punished. Though it's quite normal for younger siblings to seek acceptance from their older siblings, it wasn't normal for me to feel such an excessive need for acceptance from someone who was rejecting me. Yes, my mother scolded me for wanting to pay for acceptance but what I didn't understand was why my sister's acceptance meant so much to me or why I felt she had to like me. It was not until much later that I learned that my willingness to pay for friendship revealed a small but incredibly influential part of my character.

You would classify my family as "average." We always had more than we needed. My parents were hard working. My mom was a state worker and my dad a factory worker. Like most parents, they had their ups and downs but always took good care of my sisters and me.

Christmas was and still is my favorite holiday. I was very fortunate to receive every gift on my list every year. Something about the spirit of giving and holiday cheer always brings a smile to my face. One Christmas, I received a karaoke machine and rollerblades. Yes, I was the only rollerblading black child in the entire neighborhood. The karaoke machine unearthed my love of music and gift for song. I would sing all the time; this annoyed my sister of course but I didn't care.

My aunt was a super saint – you know, one of those people who practically live at church because they are a part of every ministry and attend every service. She would drag me along with her and I didn't mind because I loved the music. My mother loved God and went to church often as well. My father, however, had some doubts and kept quiet about his faith. By the age of thirteen, my interest and talent in music were recognized at church and I became one of the lead vocalists on the praise and worship team. I soon graduated as president of my eighth-grade class and honor student ready for the next chapter in life: high school.

The summer before high school I remember having two serious conversations with my mother. The first was about the "birds and the bees." The conversation went something like this "Don't be out there with those boys acting fast, you're too smart for that," end of conversation. I walked away with absolutely nothing.

The second conversation was about my biological father. Now this conversation was a happenstance. My mother casually revealed that the man I'd called dad for my whole life was not my biological father. This news was heartbreaking and my world crumbled as if a wrecking ball had slammed into it. I asked so many questions and received no answers. I wanted to know who it was I belonged to. My young mind was in turmoil.

That night I cried myself to sleep and woke up full of resentment and bitterness. I was broken. I was in search of the truth, feeling like a puzzle with missing pieces. I had to pick myself up and get over it. We all have our very own way of getting over things. I buried my pain in my heart and masked it behind a beautiful smile.

As a parent, communication is very important. No matter how scary or uncomfortable you may feel with the message, it's best to start the conversation and let God lead you through the rest. If you won't talk to your children about sex, drugs, alcohol, or family secrets someone or something else will. Negativity and temptation do not take days off. They are on the clock 24/7 and boldly invade the curious or confused minds. Thoughts have power. A simple lack of communication can cause a whirlwind of thoughts and ideas to form in the mind, whether true or false. If your mother or father didn't talk to you openly, break the cycle of silence with the wisdom of God and build relationships of trust and open dialogue with your children.

My mother always taught me to be confident and to love and respect myself. She always called me gorgeous, intelligent, and talented and was very proud of me. Her words emboldened my heart, they shaped me. That was her way of helping me deal with life but I was still broken and silently screaming out for help and healing. I wanted to meet my father, I asked God to help me find him. Every Sunday I would pour my heart out in praise and worship. God was my only refuge and I believed he had a plan for me.

My sophomore year in high school I met a guy who was so handsome. I had a crush on him but for some reason, we were more like friends. He asked about my father and paternal family, I didn't know much but something odd was apparent. This boy and my biological dad shared the same last name. As it turned out, he was my first cousin. He told me everything about my dad; he had answers to my many questions and I was so excited. I asked my new cousin to introduce me to my dad. I waited and waited and my cousin finally told me, "Your dad knows all about you. He said he loves you but does not want to meet you."

This was devastating. My heart filled with anger and rejection – a recipe for disaster. How can someone love you and hurt you at the same time? How could this man I had never met cause me so much pain? The moment I had found out about this man, I painted a picture of what he was like in my mind. But the actual man did not meet my expectation and I was hurt and disappointed. I never told anyone what my dad said. I buried it in my heart and carried on like everything was ok.

I continued to hear my mother's words, *You are gorgeous, I love you, hold your head up high.* With this, I was able to pull myself together but I also began to search for love and acceptance from men. At the age of sixteen, I was pregnant. My life was changed forever.

My family was nearly torn apart. My dad threatened to divorce my mom and leave us if I didn't have an abortion. I wondered how something so beautiful and innocent could cause so much chaos and family stress. In my mind abortion was not an option. I had already connected with my unborn child and was ready to embrace motherhood. I wanted to keep my baby with no help from the father of my baby. I was ready to deal with this on my own. Single teenage mother. What was I thinking? Surely this child deserved better than what I had to offer, but I thought that if God gave him to me there must be a plan. (*When things are at their worst, God is at his best* may sound clichéd but it's the truth.) That winter I gave birth to a healthy baby boy. My dad immediately fell in love with his new grandson and spoiled him rotten. He did not leave us.

One crazy thing happened when I was leaving the hospital with my new baby a nurse said to me "See you next year."

Whoa, lady! What are you talking about? She had me all wrong; no way was I going to get pregnant again! No way! One year later, I saw the same nurse that spoke those words to me. I was pregnant with my second son at the age of seventeen and had fallen into the cycle.

One in every five teen moms between the ages of fifteen and nineteen have repeat births. How did I repeat this mistake? My heart was still searching for love, I was still looking for acceptance, and I was still broken. With the odds stacked against my favor, I made a decision.

Knowing that it's how you handle the fork in the road that draws you to your purpose or away from it, I made a mental decision to stop blaming others for my mistakes. I stopped playing the victim and became the victor. I knew I had the power to change the course of my life. I still had the power to dream and see those dreams come true. I had to live the life I deserved to live and not the life people expected me to live. You are only a failure if YOU say so. When the fork in the road came again and I chose to follow my dreams and go to college.

God has made provisions for your life

One thing about a dream is that it must be aligned with actions. If you want something, go after it. I wanted to graduate college with honors. This was my dream before I even enrolled in school. I didn't have a blueprint or GPS and I didn't know how I was going to do this. I had a 1-year-old, a newborn and bull-dog faith. The college recruiter came to my house for a meeting with my parents. We discussed the curriculum and tuition. My parents told the recruiter we couldn't afford college but, thank you for your time. The recruiter looked at the disappointment on my face and then something happened. He saw my 2 boys and said, "You have some cute little brothers."

I said, "Sir, these are my children."

He said, "ARE YOU SERIOUS!?"

I said, "Yes."

The recruiter turned to my parents and said, "Because Dorothea has a family of her own and her income is

$0, she will receive every government grant available to students and teens with multiple children. Dorothea can start school this fall. Her schedule will be in the mail."

GLORY TO GOD! From that moment onward I knew I was not alone, God had already made the provision. The desires of my heart were given to me by God and they aligned with his will for my life. My challenges became faith-building opportunities to put my trust in God.

It wasn't always easy to trust God, though. One day I was on my way to praise and worship rehearsal when my car broke down. I had my two small children with me and I was stranded on the side of a road. I was 18 years old, in college full time, working part time, barely able to afford baby diapers and clothes. The pressure to succeed in school and provide for my children was overwhelming.

Trying to soothe a crying baby and type research papers was exhausting. I was lonely, afraid and screaming on the inside. I didn't have the strength to deal with car problems or anything else. I couldn't breathe. I was having an anxiety attack and the enemy began to work on my mind. I heard voices in my head that told me to jump off the bridge.

"No one will miss you. Your kids deserve better...you have nothing. Just JUMP!"

At that moment, I wanted to listen to those loud voices. They offered peace and I found myself actually wanting to jump off the bridge and die. Life had become too hard for me to bear. I was listening to the voices in my head but before I could take action, a small, still voice said, "Look up."

Tears streaming down my face, I saw a car had pulled over to help me. It was a woman who said she never stopped for people on the side of the road but for some reason, she couldn't drive past me. She offered to give me and my babies a ride. We made it to a relative's house where I asked for and got a ride to church for praise and worship. After all, that's where I needed to be. I poured my heart out at the altar. Every hurt, disappointment, and fear, and thoughts of suicide I laid at the throne of grace. I turned it all over to God.

The very next day after getting my car towed to the repair shop, there was a check in the mail with my name on it. That check was enough for a new car! God heard me, provided for me and he loves me. Trusting and waiting for God is not easy but it is worth it.

Press Forward

Some people ask, what is your biggest motivation? What is the driving force behind what you do? My answer: the people around me. I have a natural drive to be an example, to raise the standard and challenge "you can't" and "there's no way." Every negative word or thought pushed me harder to achieve positive results. Words are powerful. The brain is voice-activated - whatever thought you allow to abide in your subconscious realm becomes a conscious thought, a belief, and then an action. Negative words and thoughts must be counteracted by positivity. Mastering this is the first step to success. Get immersed in positive affirmations and daily meditation.

The people around you will either draw you closer to making your dreams a reality or pull you away. The people that draw you closer are success builders and motivators. They are successful, like-minded people who challenge you to walk in excellence even when you want to be lazy and make excuses. If you don't have a life motivator or someone to push you and encourage you, do it yourself. There is no room for excuses. Turn your excuse into your *why not* and move forward.

I used to run away from professional life coaches, mentors, pastors, or perky success builders. I used to wonder, why are they so happy ALL the time? No one is happy ALL the time. Then God started to show me the heart of a success builder; they are optimistic visionaries. Not just for themselves, but for others as well. They are goal-oriented planners and take joy in the success journey.

God began to show me the characteristics of a success builder and told me this is who I am. I had to discover the many facets of my identity and trust God to develop me into the person He wanted me to be. The reason I was running from the "vision board gang" was that they exemplified a life of discipline and focus. The biggest thing I had to deal with was the law of distraction.

You know that distractions come in many forms: social media, friends, family, co-workers. They present you with the wrong things at the right time. When you're focused, or putting the finishing touches on your vision board, or are excited about something...that's when these negative people have a better idea or know someone that tried the very same thing and it didn't work out. They are opinionated, always complaining, or need to borrow money, or hold lengthy conversations about absolutely nothing and will delay your progress. Time is valuable and should not be wasted. I remember one of my best college friends who always partied, never studied and had a good time at the expense of others. When I shared my dreams with her, she laughed and said, "There's no way; where will you get the money? Who will watch your kids? You're too young for anyone to take you seriously."

Negative words can either fuel your dream or kill your dream. I was discouraged by my friend's words and had to end our friendship. Not everyone can handle the plan God has for your life. Be mindful of dream killers and associate yourself with positive like-minded individuals who will nurture your dreams until they become a reality, no matter how long the manifestation takes.

Cherish and appreciate your supporters

My parents played a significant role in my success – my mother to be exact. She taught me everything about motherhood in words and in actions. My mother didn't care about what I said or did, she was always there. When I didn't have a car, she took my kids to daycare and make sure I had a way to school. She would babysit and help me financially.

She was dedicated to my success. When you have someone in your corner with that level of dedication, you become motivated and want to make them proud. Surrounding myself with positive people who believed in my dreams helped me to reach higher and maximize my potential.

May 2008, the Wednesday before Mother's day, my life-long supporter and number one cheerleader passed away. A surgical mistake took my mother's life. And once again I felt alone, questioning God, stricken with grief and devastated! We were best friends. She understood me, picked me up when I was falling apart and comforted me through it all. She was never ashamed and never spoke a negative word about my life.

I didn't appreciate her enough. I thought she would always be there. Sometimes I didn't even have time to sit and have dinner with her or grab a cup of coffee because I was too busy. I didn't have time to listen to her talk about how she was feeling. I only cared about what I needed. Mothers, fathers, grandparents, aunts, cousins or mentors whoever your supporters, show them how much you appreciate them TODAY because tomorrow is not promised.

Live the Life You Want to live, not the Life Others Expect You to Live

After graduating from college with honors, I started a career in digital mapping validation and quality for a global organization. Through my commitment to excellence and business process improvement, I received the American Society for Quality Lean Six Sigma Certification. I went back to school for a master's degree in business administration and placed my focus on financial success and asset protection for families. I started building my own business as a life insurance producer and international gold acquisition expert. I take pride in helping families protect their assets and plan for their future. I also mentor young men and women on the importance of basic money management, credit, financial planning and career development. I became a success because I want my children to be successful. The success journey starts with me. As I succeed I pass the baton to my children and they pass the baton to their children. It's about instilling family values and establishing a belief system for generations to come. I need to be educated and leave an inheritance I need to trail-blaze the way forward and create a legacy that my children can be proud of. If there is a generational cycle of poverty in your family, break the back of poverty. Take the responsibility and say, "It stops with me!"

There are so many people that want this but don't want to put in the work and don't want to be held accountable. Deep inside I felt there was more to me than my circumstance. I didn't want to be another negative statistic; I wanted to defy the odds. I believe God put those desires in my heart for such a time as this. The more I walked toward my dreams, God began to light up my path. As I continued to press forward, God began to remove obstacles. He made situations that seemed impossible...possible! The more I walk with God, the more my faith increases. Line upon line, precept upon precept, I moved from faith to faith and glory to glory.

There were times when I was faced with despair, discouragement, sadness, rejection or pain. That is a sign you are still human and live on earth. Instead of focusing on what's going wrong focus on what's going right. Every time I would have a pity party and cry, "Woe is me!" God would remind me of when he came through for me, of the time he worked it out for my good and when he delivered on his promise for my life.

I couldn't see the outcome of my life when I was 16

and pregnant. I didn't see my degrees, my career, and my businesses. There was no life-size GPS providing me with turn by turn navigation. Sounds really cool but it doesn't exist. God's GPS goes something like this:

"Keep straight."

"For how long God?"

No response.

"Can I stop here and take a break?"

No response.

"Can I turn right?"

No response.

"Is this thing still working?"

God's GPS goes, "Stay the course and KEEP STRAIGHT." He doesn't give you any additional details he just says, "Keep straight." I had to travel down some dark paths and trust God's plan for my life. No matter what the circumstances are, no matter how hard you may think life is, push your fears aside and know you are already a winner, you are an entrepreneur, you are debt free, you are a success, and your children are blessed.

When life takes an unexpected turn, don't lose sight of the winner's circle, the success, and the passion for change or your positive affirmations. In the midst of your circumstances, "purpose" is still alive. It has a profuse heartbeat with a sound that resonates in our hearts and minds. Your pain, disappointment, and circumstances have sounds as well. Your affirmations must be louder than your circumstances in order to silence them. Stop using this little timid voice – roar like a lion and run *at* your situation.

When you silence the sound of your circumstances and listen to the heartbeat of your purpose you begin to draw closer and closer and discover more and more. My teenage pregnancy didn't change my purpose, it added more noise. That divorce didn't change your purpose, it added more noise. Your failed business didn't change your purpose, it added more noise. What is noise? It's mental feedback. This mental feedback doesn't stop the sound of your purpose. It only makes it harder for you to hear it.

Have you ever been on the phone with someone and feedback comes out of nowhere so that you can barely hear them? It always happens when the conversation is getting really good or you're at the important part. You didn't stop talking but the feedback made it harder for you to hear the other person. That's the sound of your circumstance. The enemy knows if you can't hear it, you can't believe it. If you can't believe it, you can't apply your faith or trust God with it. Faith comes by way of hearing. Success begins in your mind. Getting to a place of mental clarity and focus by silencing the noise of your circumstances is the first step to recovery. What are you recovering? Your self-esteem, your self-image, your emotional health, your peace, your positive affirmations, your dreams that you put aside, or that business that you never started. Building a dynamic relationship with God aligns you with your purpose and stabilizes your mental clarity. That oneness with God and your purpose puts you on a path of discovery. As you move along the path of discovery things begin to line up, favor comes your way, doors open that no one can shut, you receive God's grace and it looks easy. The more you move closer, the less you are distracted by noise and the louder your purpose becomes. Then suddenly, you are at a place where "purpose" is all you hear and nothing can stand in your way. I challenge you to…

- Counteract negative thoughts with positive affirmations
- Understand that God has already made provisions for your life
- Turn your excuses into your why
- Be accountable; start pointing at you instead of others
- Draw closer to the heartbeat of your purpose

Life is full of choices. You cannot change the past but you can CHOOSE your future.

Luberta Lytle: Drive and Determination

My teenage life went from being carefree to turning into a reality check very quickly. I started my freshman year of high school in August of 1979. Things started out just fine until I met the drummer for the high school band who happened to be a senior. He made me feel special and I fell head over heels for him. This little romance went on for a little bit and then I started getting serious about this older person. Well, this did not work out too good for me, because I ended up pregnant at the age of 14.

I denied being pregnant for the first five months and then my mother suspected something was wrong. So, off to the doctor we went and this visit changed my life forever. I remember sitting in that office and being so nervous waiting for the physician to enter the room. He came in and completed his examination then broke the news to us that indeed I was pregnant. I will never forget the look on my mother's face when the doctor revealed the results. She looked surprised and disappointed all at the same time. I felt like I had truly let her down because I knew she wanted me to do something with my life and having a baby was not one of the choices. The nurse then asked if I knew my last menstrual cycle date and I said between October and November. She then gave me an approximate delivery date of August 17, 1980.

We left the doctor's office and returned home. My mother asked me if I knew who the father was and I said yes. She was not really impressed when she found out that he was a senior in high school. She thought that it would be a good idea for the families to get together and discuss this pregnancy. Then she proceeded to ask me if I would be finishing high school. I told her that it was bad enough that I had gotten pregnant and I did not want to make this situation worse by not finishing school. I also felt that my child would already be disappointed that I had gotten pregnant at an early age and not finishing high school would just put the icing on the cake. I knew it would be hard to finish, but I had the determination to obtain my high school diploma. My mother stated that she would leave the decision up to me and support me either way. She felt that I would make the right decision regarding my education.

Then, we set up a meeting with my baby's daddy's family and it did not go well. My baby's father and his dad did not believe that the child was his and they basically said it was our problem, not theirs. So, in an instant, I had to grow up quickly and take full responsibility for this unborn child. I returned back to school to finish my freshman year of high school and this became the downfall for my self-esteem.

I decided to confide in my best friend about the pregnancy. We had been friends since grade school and I just knew that she would support me. Oh, she did a complete 180 degree turn on me and this just blew my mind. She told other people about my pregnancy. She even joined the bandwagon when people started talking badly about me being pregnant at such an early age. This so-called friend decided that she did not want to be associated with someone, "Who was having a baby out of wedlock." Then, I found out that her parents felt I was a bad influence on her and they also suggested that she not be friends with me anymore. I learned really quickly that, just because someone smiles in your face, it does not mean they are your friend.

After dealing with this situation, the father of my baby decided that we needed to talk about the pregnancy. I was confused because he had already told me that he did not think that the child was his. I asked, "So please tell me what else we need to talk about?"

Well, this conversation did not go well either since he felt that I lied about him being the daddy to get his attention and so this quickly ended our little fling.

I never dreamed that being pregnant would make you feel like you had some kind of contagious disease and people would not want to associate with you. I had to really lean on my mother for support because, at this time, she was the only person I could talk to. I am truly thankful that my mother did not belittle me during this difficult time in my life. I do not know and could not imagine what I would have done if my mother had not been in my corner during this pregnancy.

I made it through my freshman year and then the doctor became concerned about my increased weight gain. He sent me for an ultrasound in June because he thought instead of having a single birth, I might be pregnant with twins. This did not sit well with me at all and I told him that if I were to be having twins, he would be taking one home with him. I was only half joking.

I was so relieved when I saw only one baby during this ultrasound and then the technician told me that I would be having a boy and probably earlier than my scheduled due date. At my next appointment, the doctor informed me that my son would be born in July instead of August.

Approximately two weeks after that appointment, I started experiencing pain in my lower back. This went on for a few days and then on one of my many trips to the bathroom I noticed something unusual in the toilet and screamed for my mother. She informed me that I had "lost my plug" and that we needed to make an appointment to see the doctor. She did not want me to give birth at home. We called the doctor's office and they got us in quickly.

I remember getting on the examination table and when the doctor attempted to exam me I screamed that it hurt. This did not sit well with my reserved mother. She informed me that there was no sense in screaming now "and I bet you did not scream when you were making this baby."

I just lay on the examination table completely embarrassed. The doctor confirmed that I had dilated but since it was my first baby, things would probably go slow. He sent us home and told me to wait until the contractions became regular and/or unbearable before I went to the hospital.

The pain continued through the night and by the next day my water broke. My mother appeared frantic at this time because she was really concerned that I would be delivering this baby at home. We arrived at the hospital and the nurse confirmed that I was in true labor. Then she told me that I must stay in the bed due to my water breaking. They applied the fetal monitor around my stomach and I heard my baby's heartbeat. I decided that I just wanted a nap and rolled over onto my side, causing one of the leads to become loose and the monitor to "flat line." I thought that I had killed my child and my mother was utterly amazed that I was trying to take a nap. Again, my reserved mother warned me that I would become pregnant again because I had not experienced true labor discomfort. I knew she loved me, but why would you wish that on somebody? Even with her making that comment she stayed at the hospital until I brought my son into the world on July 17, 1980.

My sons' father did come to the hospital just to make sure that everything with the delivery had gone okay. But he did not change his stance about the paternity or taking responsibility for his first born child. We never discussed if he would sign the birth certificate. He smiled, held his son and went on with his life.

Being a new mom required me to adjust to having

someone rely on me for all of their wants and needs. I also had to realize that being a mother meant that you are very limited in regards to a social life when you cannot find a reliable babysitter. I returned back to school with help from my mother who watched my son and I completed my next two years.

Oh, now let's talk about baby number two. Guess my mom was right about me getting pregnant again. I did finish my sophomore and junior year and then met baby father number two. He appeared in the beginning to be nothing like baby daddy number one. I think that's what made me attracted to him. We dated for a little bit and then I got pregnant again at the age of sixteen.

This pregnancy was emotionally and physically completely different than the first one. I endured some emotional issues this time which caused me to even question if I wanted to continue this pregnancy. I felt that my life would truly be turned upside down trying to raise two children at the age of sixteen and still trying to finish school. I had to pray and dig deep in my soul to determine what would be the best solution for me and my unborn child. Things between me and my baby's father caused even more stress because the relationship was not going well at the time. I had never been in a relationship where someone wanted to control and dictate your life. This relationship was not a healthy relationship, but I wanted to make it work because of the baby. It should have been a pretty simple decision to make, but each day of the pregnancy it became harder and harder trying to decide what I should do regarding the pregnancy. This stress took its toll on me and my unborn child for the first three months of my pregnancy. I actually lost weight instead of gaining weight during the first trimester. My gynecologist became very concerned regarding my drastic weight loss. I continued to go back and forth regarding making a decision with continuing the pregnancy. It became clear that the pregnancy would continue; I could not make myself terminate it. Even with everything that was happening in my life at the time, termination did not appear to be the proper choice for me and my unborn child. I had made the choice to have unprotected sex and knew the consequences of my actions.

So, after making the decision to continue the pregnancy, I started gaining weight as my doctor wanted me to do. Again, my mother supported me but the adults decided they wanted to ridicule me this time around. I remember such one incident. Our local church had a club for girls and I really wanted to join it, but the leader felt that I would be a bad influence on the rest of the group because of my two children out of wedlock. She also felt that the group would not be good for me because I really did not have a future. The leader informed some other adults and members of the group that the only thing that I would be doing with my life would be producing a child every two years. This truly hurt my feelings but gave me the determination to graduate on time from high school.

The two fathers did have something in common. They both liked having several women in their lives at one time and making stressful situations for the one pregnant with their child. In addition to dealing with the adults, I had to deal with the baby daddy not believing that this was his child. Being placed in this situation causes you to question your existence and makes you feel that nobody gives a damn about you. If my mother had not provided the support to help me endure the two pregnancies, I don't know what I would have done.

Being a teenager is hard enough, but when you throw two babies in the mix, that just adds more pressure and stress into a teenager's life. This pregnancy showed me again what my classmates and adults really thought of me. I had to listen to people make comments and judge me for being pregnant again.

Although it had occurred again, I still had the drive and determination to finish high school. My senior year started in August and my baby was due in November. My counselor thought that it would be best for me to stay home for the first semester of school and return at the end of Christmas break. I took my counselor's advice and enrolled in a correspondence course to receive additional credits, ensuring that I would be able to graduate in the spring.

I successfully completed my correspondence course before my other son was born in November of 1982. This delivery went a lot smoother and quicker than the first delivery. I had been in labor for a few days but never said anything to my mom because she had already told me that she did not want for this baby to be born at home either.

The pain in my lower back had become pretty intense during the middle of the night, so I got up, took a shower, then proceeded to make myself more presentable for the hospital trip and my mother woke up.

She asked me why I had gotten up so early. I told her that it might be time for us to go to the hospital. She then asked me how long I had been hurting. I said, "Oh for a couple of days, but it got really bad last night."

She jumped up and told me that nobody would care what I looked like in the delivery room. So, we left our house for the hospital. I actually had an appointment that day and thought that maybe I could have made it to the appointment instead of going to the hospital. Guess my mother was right, because the bundle of joy showed up before the scheduled gynecologist appointment. I had my second son on November 20, 1982.

The father of my second child came to the hospital to meet his son and then he informed me that he didn't want his son to have his last name. He said he didn't want to be stuck with the hospital bill. This is not something that you want to hear after having just given birth. The paperwork was completed and my son received my last name. The father claimed to care for me and wanted to build a relationship with me. How can you want to have a future with someone, but not want your first born son to have your last name because you are afraid that you might have to take on the responsibility of a hospital bill? I thought that most men would want their sons to have their last name to ensure that their name is carried on. This didn't help my self-esteem at all. I felt that all I was good enough for was to have sex with and produce a baby but not good enough for the man's child to have his last name. I got over that pretty quick and realized that I had two children that would be raised by a single teenage mother.

I returned back to school after the Christmas break but most of my classmates felt that, since I had just showed up at school, I would not be graduating with them in the spring of 1983. School proved to be more challenging this time, however, than with the first pregnancy. Yes, my mother did help take care of my children, but sometimes my babies did not care that mom had to attend school.

I remember one time during my senior year when my oldest son was sick and fussy during the night. My mom did not rush into the bedroom to check on us but let me attempt to handle the situation on my own and by the time she came into the room she found me and my son crying. She just looked at me and took him into her room. I did go to sleep and went to school the next morning.

I did receive some help from this baby's dad, but at

times it felt like more of a control issue than support. Our relationship continued off and on over the next few years. It never really amounted to anything because other women always seemed to be in the picture, too.

My youngest son spent the first six months of his life in and out of the hospital. He suffered with a lot of respiratory problems requiring him to be placed in oxygen tents and needing strong antibiotics to fight off his infections. At one point his pediatrician wanted to insert a tube in his airway to help him breathe better. I didn't like that idea and requested a second opinion. We went to the Children's Hospital in St. Louis and the doctor suggested that we continue with the current antibiotic regimen and hold off on inserting the tube. I was glad to hear this because I really didn't want my baby to endure that surgery. After six months, he outgrew all of his medical problems and started developing. This meant a lot of sleepless nights, but this is the price you pay when you are a parent.

During the school year, my classmates held several fundraisers for the end of the school-year trip and I helped out with the fundraisers. The class finally revealed that they would be going out of town and spending the night at a hotel.

I explained all the details regarding this to my mother. She informed me that I would not be attending this event if my children could not attend. I had to remember that everyone in the class did not have additional responsibilities and could go as they pleased. I did not attend the trip and again realized the reality of being a teenage mother.

During all of this time I continued to keep my grades up and finally in May of 1983, I graduated from high school. It was a wonderful feeling to see my mother and two sons sitting in the audience cheering their mother on when the principal called my name to accept my diploma. I felt very proud of myself for accomplishing this goal on time.

My life has caused me to question my relationship with people and God. I have always been raised to treat people the way I want to be treated. When you treat people in a good manner and they just step all over you then what are you supposed to do?

This caused me to close myself off and suspect everyone of wanting to cause me harm. I would not allow myself to become close to anyone, including my children. I did not know how to express love to them. It is one thing being a parent, but another thing to express love. I had the material-istic part down. I could provide material things for them, but I could not provide the nurturing and loving part of being a parent. It should have been easy for me because I had experienced love from my own parent but I could not give the same kind of love to my own children. In this area I felt as though I had failed my children.

On the other hand, I felt that my immaturity and life experiences played a major part in why I could not express love for my children. You do not get a parenting book. You must learn things through trial and error. If you are a broken child, you can turn into a broken adult. Then, over the years, I learned how to love myself and I was able to start showing love to my sons.

If a person does not feel good about themselves, they can cause damage to anyone who enters into their life. I had to realize that I could determine the final outcome of my life and that I could decide how to perceive the challenges that I have experienced on my life's journey. The obstacles have been challenging and maybe the results could have been different but overall, the challenges have made me the woman that I am today.

Yes, I could have just stayed miserable and unhappy because of the circumstances that occurred in my life. Instead, I decided to accept responsibility regarding my own actions and to grow as a result of those actions. I did not want to stay the broken child that had become the broken adult.

Life is a learning experience. I elected to take every negative experience and turn it into something positive. When, I got pregnant with my first child at the age of fourteen I could have elected to give up on life, but I decided to press on. Then it happened again at the age of sixteen and I became the every-two-year-baby-making machine. But I pressed on and still graduated even though I had become pregnant twice during my high school years. At first, I had difficulty expressing love to my children because of past relationships but I made myself learn how to love them unconditionally.

I did not like being on welfare and relying on the State of Illinois to issue me a monthly welfare check. Instead, I applied *for* a job with the State of Illinois. I wanted to be able to provide for my children. I decided after several years of being a Mental Health Technician that I deserved a different position. I signed up for college and obtained my

Practical Nursing certificate. I applied for a nursing position and received another higher paying position. It took some time but I did return back to college and eventually received my Bachelor of Science degree. Completing and receiving my Bachelor of Science degree increased my employment options with the State of Illinois. I applied for and received my current job working under the job title of Qualified Intellectual Disabilities Professional. Then I decided that I wanted more education and returned back to college one more time and obtained my Master of Business degree. I can retire from the State of Illinois in approximately two years.

My next chapter in life has already begun. I am the CEO and founder of LL Life Coaching. I work with middle-aged women who are stuck and unsatisfied in their current professional and personal life. This new chapter will bring joy and satisfaction in my life because I am able to help women overcome their obstacles and fears to start living the life they have always desired. I have always been told that when I set my mind to accomplishing something, I do not stop until I have accomplished it. I know that with drive and determination, I will continue to be successful in all of my endeavors.

Well, I am still living and guess I need to establish some more goals. I am determined to have the best life that I can give myself, friends, loved ones and anybody else that I encounter along my life's journey. My life has truly been a roller coaster ride and I have enjoyed the ride.

This is how I live my life: If you do not like something in your life, change it or quit complaining about it. You determine the outcome of your life. Choose a life of happiness and success instead of sadness and despair. Life is entirely too short to just sit on the sidelines and watch it pass you by. You only get one life, so make the most of it, because you will not get the chance to repeat it. Instead of continuing to play the victim role, become victorious over your life and live life to its fullest.

LaKeisha Stringfellow: Facing Your Fears

"For I know the plans that I have for you declares the Lord, Plans to prosper you and not harm you, plans to give you a future and a hope"

-Jeremiah 29:11(NIV)

You are an Overcomer. You are Victorious. You are Strong. You are Loved. You are Healed. You are Free. You do have Morals. You can accomplish Your Goals. What are you afraid of? What is holding you back? Do you feel trapped because you were or are a teen-aged Mom? Who do you have in your corner? Are you asking people for help?

Affirmations, questions, what is it all about? Glad you asked. My name is LaKeisha Stringfellow, and I am YOU! I am the product of a teen-aged mother and I was a teen-aged mother. I found what I needed to move forward and no longer be afraid and now I am here to help you do the same. I hope that you take this short journey with me through this chapter and read a little about my story so that you will be inspired, uplifted and encouraged to *Face your Fears*.

From a very young age, I knew that I wanted to be a

wife and a mother. As a product of a single teen-aged mom, I was given the responsibility to care for my two small siblings at the age of twelve. I have a brother who is four years younger than I and I also have a sister who is ten years younger. I have two other siblings, but they came along later. Yes, my mom was busy! I was not sure for a very long time why I wanted the task of having a family and children at such an early age, but I did. I later found out, it was because of my desire for family and unity! I met a boy at age fifteen and fell in love with him...or at least what my perception of love was at that age. We were in a relationship for 7 years. I got pregnant three times by him. The first two pregnancies ended in miscarriages and the third time, around the age of eighteen, I had a full term, healthy baby boy.

I wasn't at all afraid of what having a baby while young would be like. I had a very strong support system. My family, although not happy with the fact that I was pregnant so young, supported me. His family, without a shadow of a doubt, supported us. His mom was super excited to be a granny (may she rest in peace). So, having no support was the least of my worries.

The only thing that I could remember being afraid of

was the thought of not being a good mother to my son. I wanted to do everything to nurture and care for him. I'd decided my senior year of high school that I didn't want to go to college. I initially wanted to join the US Navy, but that idea was quickly tossed to the side when I found out that because of my military exam score, I would not be able to go into nursing. Instead, I would do what I knew best. Go to work and make an honest living.

I mentioned nursing because it was a HUGE dream of mine. My love and passion for people are what gave me the desire to want to see people whole and healed. But of course, over time, that dream began to quickly fade away. How could I become a nurse? I didn't want to even go to college. I was afraid of college. I didn't think that I was good enough, plus who would pay for it? My parents were not financially able to send me to college. So, that's why I'd decided that college wasn't for me. Let's be clear. I had NO love for school whatsoever. Anyway, after high school, I had a son that I needed to financially care for and felt there was no time for college.

Well, here we were, my son's father and I happily

together with our first son, his namesake. I wanted so desperately to be married to complete my little family. I was brought up in the church and living in sin was not on my "things to do list." But as in love as I thought we were, my son's father wasn't ready to marry me. And, to be honest, it wasn't a part of God's plan for my life. I know that now, but you couldn't have told me that back then. Needless to say, my son's father and I broke up. I was now twenty-one years old, almost twenty-two and a single, single mom, if you get where I am coming from. I still had the support of both families, but it wasn't the same.

After my break-up with the "love of my life," I was devastated. I didn't think that I would be able to make it without him. After all, we'd been together for seven years. What was I going to do now? Who was I going to marry? Who would help me raise my boy? I felt like my world was ending. I began a life of out-of-control living and behavior. I knew God and had been saved, but being a backslider was an understatement. I did everything under the sun. Anything that you can imagine, I probably did it. I had absolutely NO SHAME. Or at least, I thought that there was "no shame in my game."

I hopped from relationship to relationship. I drank, smoked weed, hung out at all times of the night and was extremely promiscuous. All of those things were really connected to the abuse that I had endured as a young child. But, that's another story that you'd have to read about in my next book (*PLUG!*). Now, I was no longer a teenager, but I still had the mentality of one. Goals, what goals? Dreams, what dreams? I had nothing. The only thing that I became concerned with was where I was going to hang out and who was going to keep my kids. Yes, in the midst of all the madness, at the age of twenty-two, I had my second son. And yes, you guessed it, by a different guy.

I had met this guy and we instantly clicked. We did everything together. We were joined at the hip. What I wasn't prepared for was the physical abuse that I would sustain in the relationship. Things moved very quickly, this time around. I still knew that I wanted to be married and have a family. But if you are a believer in Christ, you must know that you cannot do things your way, right? Still, I had a plan for my life. Notice that I said *I*. Pregnant two months into this new relationship and I convinced myself that I loved him. What was I desperate for? What was I longing for?

Love. He was very abusive and fought with me on many occasions during our year and a half long relationship. I won't talk about him much, though. It ended and I am still here, Thank God.

Here is the meat of what you need to know and what I really want you to get out of reading this chapter: Just because your life didn't go as planned, just because you had a baby at an early age, that doesn't count you out. Making wrong decisions is very much a part of your growth process. Would your life be different if you'd chosen not to birth a child at an early age? Probably, but how so? Don't dwell on your past. You have to learn to forgive yourself and move forward. Forgiving yourself is not an easy task, but you must start there in order to achieve your goals and dreams. You have to believe that you can do it and that you are worth it. Because you are. Look in the mirror and encourage yourself. No really, put this book down, go look in the mirror and tell yourself that you are worth it. Tell yourself to fight for what you want to accomplish.

For years, I struggled. My mom called me a vagabond. So I made a vow to myself that I would not make my children feel unstable, moving from here to there, staying with anyone and everybody and transferring them from school to school. Well, I made this vow to myself AFTER I'd indeed lived from here to there lugging my boys around anywhere and everywhere. But I grew tired and weary. Because of the God in me, I knew that there had to be a better life for my sons and me.

After those many years of getting it all wrong and being in a whirlwind, I decided that I needed to make some changes. I went back to school and obtained my degree. I needed to find a better job and become stable and capable of taking care of my two boys on my own.

Please note that when you finally decide to make a change, it will not come easy. There will be many obstacles and hurdles, but you will overcome. You have to continue to remind yourself of why. Why you want to change, why you want to be different, and why your children deserve better than what you had. You owe it to yourself to be the best you that you can be. If you don't begin to take care of yourself, you will never be any good to your children, even with all of your best efforts and intentions.

I got back to my real first love, God. I rededicated my life to Christ and committed myself to being an active member of my church. I'd finally gotten what I thought was my dream job working at The University of Chicago Medical Center. My boys and I were finally a bit more stable than we'd ever been. We moved into our very first apartment that had our names on the lease – something we could call our own. They were happy. But I still wasn't. Don't get me wrong. I was happy for them now that they finally had some stability. But something was missing for me. I worked at the University for eight and a half years and I left there the first opportunity I got.

By then, I was married to a loving and nurturing husband of almost seven years. We had two more children in the home and my life seemed to be doing great. But there was still something missing. I became very bitter and unhappy with life. I was angry all the time and I lashed out at my kids and my husband. I felt unfulfilled and was still seeking to find my place. What was it that I should be doing? Who was I? I had no clue. I had gone through so many things in my life but never stopped to find out what was going to make LaKeisha happy. It was time to do some self-reflecting and figure out what it was that was holding me back from reaching my full potential.

I began to pray and do some soul searching. I needed to know what God had in store for me. I knew what Keisha wanted but what were those gifts in me that needed to reach the world? The word of God in, 3 John 1:2 says, "Beloved, I wish above all things that thou mayest prosper and be in health, even as thy soul prospereth,"(KJV). So, knowing that and the vision and the dreams that God had given me from early on, I knew that there was more. There was, for me, more than being a wife and a mom. Those things are great, and I am grateful and thankful that I finally had them both, but there was still more. I had to face my fears. There were some things keeping me from reaching my full potential. There were some things that I was holding onto from my past. It was time to let go and excel.

Here we go. It was now March of 2015. I'd met a woman at my friends' church who was a fashion designer and stylist. We connected, exchanged information (because you must know that I am a fashionista!) and got together to talk about an event that she was planning. When I told her some of my interests, she asked me to be a part of the event. I was super excited, still not knowing why God had put this beautiful sister in my path. Well, the event never happened. But one day, she did call me and asked me to model at an event that she was styling and for which she was doing a fashion show. I agreed, although I had never modeled before in my life. I had always been told that I should have been a model, so hey, maybe this would be my "Big Break..." *HAHAHA!* The stylist told me that I would love this event. I was in direct sales by this time and she thought that my product would be great and that I would be able to do some networking.

So, there I was, the day of the event that changed my life FOREVER. All it takes is one moment for God to shift everything in your life. When you have made up your mind to do something different and begin to seek it out, it will come. When you begin to speak positive affirmations about your life and start to believe what you are saying, you will begin to see the open doors and endless possibilities. I am a firm believer that when you start praying and seeking God, He hears you and He answers you. It is up to us to listen and walk according to His will. And even if you are a non-believer, I truly believe that it all works the same. What you speak and do, will come back to you, be it positive or negative. Ok, so back to this life-changing event.

The title of the event was "Rock Your Royalty." I

had no expectations because I had no clue what the event was about. I just knew that a bunch of women would be there, there would be a fashion show and I would model and get a free meal and maybe do a bit of networking…sounded good enough to me!

I was sitting at a table of about eight women whom I didn't know. The woman directly to my right was very friendly. She told me how great the event would be and how awesome the women all were and she was right. I was totally amazed at all of the positive energy in the room. I had never, and I do mean *never*, experienced a sisterhood so strong in my entire life. I was surrounded by nothing but genuine love. You know how you walk into a room full of women and you get the instant stares and up-and-down looks – checking you out, so to speak? I experienced none of that. I was in awe. All of the speakers were amazing and I just remember thinking, "Wow, I wish I had the courage to be strong to minister to women."

After that event, I pretty much Facebook friended most of the women that I could remember. I made up in my mind to stay in the presence of the powerful woman that was the host of these events. Since I had been praying for a move from God, a change, and a clear direction for my life, I was sure I would find what it was that I needed to be doing to fulfill my dreams and goals. Remember those dreams that I had let die because I became a mother so young? But now something was stirring in me. So, I followed this woman and, wherever she was, I told myself, *there I would be*. I just kept hearing that I needed to invest in me. I needed to grow and become stronger and more confident in who I was and what I was and was to become.

Let's fast forward a couple of months to somewhere mid-summer, 2015. The same woman that held the "Rock Your Royalty" event was hosting another event entitled, "Butterfly Brunch." This more intimate brunch gave me the opportunity to meet more like-minded women. I actually sat at a table with Ms. Alicia Bowens and four other women during this event. They all talked about their companies and the projects that they were working on. I remember Alicia even speaking about this very book project that you are reading right now and thinking to myself, *Man, I would love to be a part of that!* I knew that I had a story to tell and had even considered writing a book. But for many years, fear crippled me. Each of the ladies talked about what they were working on and what was next, and then it was my turn. They wanted to know about me. *WHAT?* Umm…I felt ashamed. After all, I was only a housewife and working at a place that nobody even knew about. All eyes were on me but to my surprise, as I belittled myself, these women uplifted me. They began to ask me questions like, "Well, what is it that you want to do? What are some of your goals?" Then they started pointing out people that I should connect with. Can you say NETWORKING? My eyes were being opened.

I finally connected with that beautiful and anointed woman that I was telling you about. Her name is Priscilla Williams. She has been such a blessing in my life. Through her mentoring program, I discovered how to stand strong. I am now no longer walking in fear. I am not saying that I never get afraid, but I have learned that even when I am scared out of my mind, I do it anyway. Whatever the "it" is. Fear has a way of stopping you in your tracks but only if you allow it to. I decided that I was not going to let fear stop me.

I have been setting goals, affirming myself every day, and my prayer life has gotten stronger. I had to forgive myself for past mistakes. I had to forgive other people in my life. Not forgiving others and myself were causing me to be stagnant and I believe that it also caused fear to be a very strong factor in my life. Afraid to take chances. Afraid that I wasn't good enough. Afraid of what other people would think of me. But guess what? None of that matters when you walk fearlessly.

The people that you are supposed to touch, you will. The things that you are supposed to do, you will do. When you become fearless, you become unstoppable and the sky truly is the limit. Fear is an emotion and you have to know that you have control over your emotions. The word of God in 2 Tim 1:7 says, "For God did not give us a spirit of timidity (fear), but a spirit of power, of love and of self-discipline," (NIV). So where does this fear come from? It comes from the things that you have heard. It comes from failures and rejection. But you must know that you have the wherewithal to move past your fears. Don't let your dreams and visions die because of fear. Someone is waiting for you to become great. Someone will have hope because you were able to walk through your fears and face your goals. All it takes is one thought. Will you choose to change the way that you think about your circumstance?

When I made a conscious decision to change my

thinking and elevate my thoughts, everything around me began to change. I am now doing what I love. I am reaching women and girls and helping them to reach their goals. And this all started because I decided that I wanted more and that I deserved more. I got comfortable with what, who and *whose* person I am. When you become confident, nothing and no one will be able to stop you from reaching your goals.

Will there be days of uncertainty? There most certainly will be. But, you have the power to change your world. No one can stop you but you. You are more than a conqueror. You are Bold. You are Successful. You are reaching your goals. You do have a vision. You are Strong and able to do great Exploits. You are worth it. You have what it takes. You no longer walk in fear. Remember that someone is waiting for you. Visualize it, write it down, speak it, and walk in it. Be blessed my Sister. And remember that I AM YOU!

Millionaire *M.O.M.* Challenge #2

"Sometimes the hardest part of the journey is believing you're worthy of the trip."

-Glenn Beck

Everything you need in order to achieve your dreams is already inside of you. Surrounding yourself with people who will help you to bring out those gifts is key. Find an upcoming event or support group in your area of interest. Attend the next meeting or event.

Reflect on the following questions:

1. How did it feel to be around people who shared the same interests as you? Were they supportive?
2. What new information did you learn? Would you attend another meeting/event?

III. MY DREAMS ARE WORTH FIGHTING FOR

---

*Blessed is she who has believed that the
Lord would fulfill His promises to her."*

— *Luke 1:45*

I believe in the dreams for my life. I know if the vision was placed in my head, then it is possible for me to bring it to fruition. I write down my dreams and create a plan of action to make those dreams come true. I am ok if others do not understand my dreams and I move forward in faith.

Conchetta Jones: A Letter to My Sis

Dear Lil Sis,

I really had a hard time coming up with a message to share with you about my experience as a teen mom. I actually wrote four different drafts but tore up each one.

They just did not seem to convey the message I wanted to share with you about that time in my life, so many years ago. While my pregnancy was not a horrible experience, it did give me moments of envy, fear, and self-doubt. I do not want to make it seem like being a teen mom was a breeze, but I also do not want you to think that because you are a teen mom, your life is over or that you won't be able to follow your dreams for your life.

See, I became a teen mom at age sixteen. My son was born twenty-nine days before my 17th birthday. During that time, I experienced many different experiences and emotions. First, I did not believe I was pregnant. I imagined all kinds of reasons why I was not getting my period.

So denial played a big role. I think I just thought I could wish my pregnancy away. That is how our minds work at that age. We think things can happen to other people but not to us.

I started having sex around the same time as three of my close friends. I can remember the day my friend told me that she had had sex with her boyfriend. I was surprised. Up until that day I had not thought seriously about having sex and we used to talk about the girls that we knew who were.

My friend really thought she was in love. I remember when she and her boyfriend broke up and she cried for a week. Her boyfriend was her world. She didn't eat and it was horrible. I didn't know what to say to console her. I would just nod my head and try to look sympathetic. I think I was happier than she was when they got back together.

But anyway she was the first to admit to having sex. She said they had gotten "restless" and it had happened. So, that became our code name for having sex: *getting restless*. As each one of us started having sex we would share with the others that we had gotten restless. I think I was the last one to get "restless." Not surprisingly, we each got pregnant in the order that we had started having sex.

So even though back in those days it was not popular

to be pregnant while still in school, it was not so bad, because I had my friends. Back then a girl in that situation had to get permission from the school board to stay in school.

I can still remember the day that my Aunt Dot went up to the school with me. I was living in Mobile, Alabama at that time. I had moved down south to go to high school. I sat there silent as she spoke with the Principal and signed the papers that allowed me to remain in school.

My pregnancy experience was not all that bad. I only had morning sickness once. I didn't start showing until I was six months. I never had to really buy maternity clothes and instead just bought pants a little larger and wore big tops. Back then it was not how it is today. You did not wear cute clothes that fit your stomach. Everything had to be big and flowing. So, in my big baggy tops, I didn't feel fashionable at all.

I was not fat but I had that round basketball stomach. I used to get really bad cramps in my legs at night. They would wake me up and my calves would be sore the next morning.

I also had crazy food cravings like burnt bologna

cooked directly on the fire and then eaten with bread and barbeque sauce and Milky Way candy bars. These are things I had to have daily. And suddenly I hated one of my favorite meals – mac and cheese. Just the smell of it would make me sick.

My family did not find out I was pregnant until I was six months. Once I shared with the family that I was pregnant, my uncle said that he knew it all the time. He said he could tell by the second pulse in my neck. What? Is that some southern old wives' tale?

Before that time, I had spent days contemplating running away. Where I would go, I did not know. I can remember thinking about getting on the Greyhound bus and just riding. I just knew that I did not want to tell my mom that I was pregnant.

I thought about getting an abortion but in those days they were not as acceptable or as easy to get as they are today. They say that you are not supposed to take laxatives when you are pregnant. Well, I took lots of Ex-Lax. I don't even know if they still make that stuff. But it looked like a chocolate candy bar.

Needless to say, it did not terminate my pregnancy. I just spent a lot of time in the bathroom. There was a woman that was supposed to "fix" those things. I didn't know who she was but I had heard the gossip.

While I wanted to go see this woman, I was afraid. I didn't know what to expect and I didn't know anybody I could ask.

I remember the day we told my folks that I was pregnant. It was a phone call. We walked down to the drugstore and there was a phone booth outside. My boyfriend told my dad. He was sweating bullets as he said, "Mr. Boose, I don't know if this is good news or bad, but Connie is pregnant."

Both my dad and mom took it better than I expected. My mom had always said that if one of her girls got pregnant that she was going to put her out. So I had been afraid of that. But my mom was very supportive during that time.

My dad had great insurance – Blue Cross Blue Shield. I had a wonderful, caring ob/gyn and a private room when I delivered my son, who arrived two weeks early. The hospital stay in those days was four days.

The day I delivered my little boy, I will never forget.

I woke up with this strong urge to go to the bathroom, but I didn't make it. I thought I had wet the bed. My water bag had broken.

A visit to the doctor confirmed that I would be having my baby before the night was over. I had plans to go to a Parliament/Funkadelic concert the next day. I even had a new "maternity" outfit to wear. It was a gift from one of my friends.

I had never been as afraid as I was when I got to the hospital and my aunt could not go upstairs with me. It was not like it is now, where the family can hang out with you. Back then you were on your own. My aunt Dot and my boy-friend could only go as far as the bank of elevators.

Once there, the nurse pushed my wheelchair into the elevator and up we went. On our floor, I heard women screaming from down the hall and I just wanted to run back out of the hospital. I was terrified and felt like the baby could just stay in me forever. I had heard about labor pains, but now I was hearing with my own ears and I did not want any part of it.

All in all, the experience was not too terrible. They

gave me something to start my labor, because I had not had a pain yet, and when the pains got too bad after about 3 hours, they gave me something to sleep.

I say I went to sleep. People tell me that I couldn't have been asleep because I would have needed to be awake to push. Whatever they gave me made me not remember anything. When I woke up my son had been in the world two hours. He was beautiful.

During my pregnancy, I had only thought about having a girl. I had her name all picked out and would write it on my tablets daily while sitting in class. I was so disappointed when they told me in the delivery room that I had a boy. Since I had only planned on having a girl I didn't even have a boy's name picked out.

But when I saw my beautiful baby all my disappointment melted away. I remember saying, "Ooh he's so pretty, I don't care that I have a boy." He had a head full of hair and looked like a doll.

Do you know that back then, my son had to have my last name? Even though my boyfriend was right there, it was not allowed. He could not sign the birth certificate. We had to change his last name later after we married.

I didn't go back to school after my son was born, even though I had all intentions of doing so. My boyfriend and I got married and I began life as a mother and wife.

I missed out on my prom, class trip, and graduation. Those are some experiences that I regret not being a part of. I ended up getting a GED a year later. While my friends were preparing for college, I was tending house.

People in my family watched me closely for the first month or two because I had never been a fan of children. They wanted to make sure I was bonding with my son. And guess what? I was.

My son was treated like a little king. He had a schedule. He woke up at a certain time, had story time, park time, snack time, etc. He changed clothes three times a day. Every time he spilled something on his outfit I changed him. He was lotioned and powdered.

My brothers-in-law used to make fun of me for treating him like a girl. I soon relaxed and let him get dirt on him without me running to clean him up. He was very advanced. He walked at 8 months and was potty trained at about 14 months. If I have to say so myself, I was a pretty good mother. ☺

My marriage lasted 5 years. We were just too young. But because my dad said I had to come back to Chicago once the baby was born, we decided to get married. I did not want to go back to Chicago and leave my boyfriend.

Anyway, soon married life became too much. I got tired of having to clean and cook dinner. I just wanted to go out and do things like my friends. But finding a babysitter was always my job.

My husband continued to hang out with his friends. He soon started hanging out with his buddies at the frat house. He was there all the time. He would come home from work, eat dinner and head to the frat house. He would even travel to visit friends at Alabama State and Alabama A&M.

He soon started seeing someone else and our marriage ended. Even though our marriage did not last, he has always been a great father. He was always there and a great provider.

He actually kept my son from the age of ten. I had moved to Meridian, MS at that time and was getting ready to move to Philadelphia. He asked me not to take his son away from him.

I had been having issues being a single mom around that time. Some older boys had been picking on my son and when I went out to "get" them, they were all bigger than me. Even though they did not disrespect me and they left my son alone, I thought about what would have happened if they hadn't.

Another time I sent my son to the store and he came back crying. Some bigger boys had scared him with their dog. I think it was a Doberman. Well, you know me. I went running down that street and up on their porch. I said some very ugly things to the boys and was ready to fight. Again, the boys were bigger than I was.

At the time I didn't care. But after the fact, I realized that I could have been in danger. The last straw was when my son wanted to join the Cub Scouts. I was the only mother there. It was not like it is now where women play a big part in the Scouts.

So, when my son said that he wanted to go back to Mobile with his dad and his friends, I let him. My son then started visiting me during the summer months and I would go visit him during Spring Break.

While my pregnancy experience was not really terrible, there were times when I felt ugly, fat, and self-conscious about being pregnant. When I was out, people would often stare at me. It was obvious I was too young to be having a baby.

I still wore my hair in two ponytails. I had to stop cheering on the pep squad, stop dancing on the dance team, stop hanging out at teen activities. Nobody said I had to stop hanging out but I just felt out of place.

These girls were talking about their latest boyfriend and hanging out. I was dealing with washing clothes, cleaning house, cooking and grocery shopping for a family of three on very little money.

While none of my friend's moms were mean to me or ever said anything ugly to me, they did not allow their daughters to babysit. I was free to visit but when I left, my son left with me even though, when I was pregnant, all my friends said they would babysit. I spent a lot of time with my Aunt Dot and her friends.

My getting pregnant was a big disappointment to my family. They had big hopes for me. I was going to be a nurse, dancer, and a writer. In school, I was usually on the honor roll and in advanced classes. I read everything I could get my hands on. So when I became pregnant all those hopes were dashed. I will never forget when my dad expressed how disappointed he was that I did not get my education. So it was always my dream to finish college in order to make my dad proud.

I finally made that dream a reality and he was at both of my graduations – when I got my Bachelors Degree in 2010 and then my master's degree in 2012. I don't know who was smiling the biggest, he or I.

Now when we're out he will tell a total stranger that I'm his oldest baby and that I have my master's degree from Governors State. I'm surprised he remembers the name of the school.

I have fulfilled most of the things that I set out to do. My journey was not as easy as it would have been if I had not gotten pregnant. My life and the things I accomplished took much longer. I went to college but it took me years to finish.

I had to take classes around my job schedules. Sometimes I could only take one class in a semester. But I was determined to get my degrees. It is so hard trying to study and write research papers when you have worked all day long. It is so hard to have to take night classes when you have been on your job since 7:30 in the morning. I can remember pinching myself to stay awake in class some evenings. I would sometimes eat candy – the sugar kept me awake.

Sometimes people discount you when they find out you were a teen parent. They look down their noses and often don't want their daughters around you. They act like it will rub off.

I hope, Lil Sis, that your journey as a teen mom has not been too bumpy. Know that while it may be hard, your determination will be worth it when you reach your goals. I advise you to get a strong network of people around you. I had a strong support system; My mom, my Aunt Dot, my cousin Fran, my Grandmom Effie, my Grandmom, Charlie Belle, my friend Kathy, and her mom. Make sure that you get people who are there to help you fulfill your dreams.

Listen to them when they give you advice. It might not be what you want to hear, but know that it is for your own good. You might feel like you are a grown woman because you are a mother. But you really aren't.

I say to listen to these people who have more wisdom than you. Also, don't think that you can't accomplish everything you had planned. You can. Like I said earlier, it may take you longer and you may have to work harder, but it can be done.

Write down your goals and post them where you can see them daily. Do not think badly of yourself and do not talk negatively about yourself. You are special and can do anything you set your mind to do.

Write down some affirmations and say them aloud daily. Journal! That was always a release for me. I used to write down my frustrations, my hopes, and my dreams.

One last thing I want to share with you, Lil Sis…Love your baby. Remember he or she did not ask to be here. That was your choice and actions. So treat your baby like the precious gift he or she is.

I have worked with young girls who were teen mothers and it was sad to see them not bonding with their babies. There will be times when you will be tired. There will be times when you will be sleepy. There will be times when you want to do something and can't because you can't find a babysitter or don't have the money because you have to buy baby stuff.

During those times take a deep breath, walk away, and call someone in your support system. Do not ever harm your baby because you are feeling inadequate or unloved. (You know, "Some kind of way.") There is a chance that the baby's father is no longer in your life. DO NOT take that out on the baby.

Even if your child looks exactly like his or her father and it hurts your soul to look at him or her, suck it up. That is just one of the consequences of your life now. Also, do not get mad because the father does not want to be with you and try to keep the baby from him. That is unfair to him and to the baby and one day you will regret it. A child needs to know the love of a father. And if the young man wants to stand up and share the responsibility, then you get out of the way. It's not about you at this point.

I went through that stage when my husband and I broke up. I was angry. When my son would ask for his dad I would say, your daddy died in the war. My Aunt Dot heard me say that one day and let me have it.

You better believe I corrected my conversation quickly. My Aunt Dot never really got mad. She was always sunshine sweet. But what I said made her mad. I also remember once I called my mom and was complaining because I wanted to do something but couldn't because I couldn't find a babysitter.

I told my mom how tired I was and that I just wanted to have some fun. I was really singing the blues. I remember her saying, "It's ok. Just remember, every day he gets bigger. He is learning to do things on his own and this time next year, you won't have to do that."

She was right. Once they get potty trained and can feed and dress themselves, you never have to do it again. But I want to tell you that one day you will find yourself wishing your baby would sit still so you can hold him or her close to you again.

My son is a grown man now with two children of his own. He owns his own Barber Shop. He is a wonderful father, making sure that he spends time with his boys. He is the child of a teen mother and I could not be more proud of him. He was not a teen parent and well into his twenties before he had his first child. His children are by the same woman who is his wife.

We proved to the world that just because I was a teen mom he was not a statistic.

Final Thoughts...

Becoming a teen mother was not what I planned to be. I had always wanted to be a journalist and a dancer. I wanted to be one of the dancers on the Carol Burnett show, and then a Solid Gold dancer.

You have probably never heard of them. But I can tell you that in those days, the Solid Gold dancers were hot.

When I became a mother and then a wife, my life as I knew it and as I had planned it, changed. I was thrown into a grown-up world in which I really did not fit. But, I no longer fit in my teenage world either. I think not knowing where I fit in played a big part in my lack of confidence at times. Because I really didn't fit in, I didn't know how to act in either world.

143

Because of the early motherhood and marriage, I always say that I finished college on the 30-year plan. Even though my education was delayed, it was always on my mind. I knew that I was going to be somebody. I didn't know how at the time, I just had that feeling.

I used to always feel like I was a few steps behind. As my friends went away to college, got good jobs and lived great lives, I was stuck in one dead end job after the other. I lived in a shabby apartment on a block of other shabby apartments. They were white, wooden, two-story apartments. The landlord was a slumlord and I was often embarrassed when people came to visit. I remember once I pretended not to be home when some co-workers stopped by uninvited. I was too ashamed to let them see my apartment. I had been to one of their homes and it was new and nicely decorated. They had all of the latest appliances.

But I continued to promise myself that it would not always be this way. My first car was a blue and black Ford LTD. It was a piece of junk and I remember once when my cousin, a friend and I were headed to my aunt's house. The car ran hot and every two blocks we had to stop and put water in it to let it cool down.

We didn't have a lot of money, so I did not have a lot of clothes or shoes. How ironic was it that I got a job at the Merry Go Round clothing store in the mall? While all of the other clerks wore stylish clothes I wore pretty simple things. I had one pair of shoes that I wore to work.

One of the ladies asked me why I always wore the little "orthopedic" shoes to work all the time. I was so embarrassed because she was one of the sharpest dressers who I never saw wearing the same thing twice.

We got shipments in every week and she would buy things every time. I laughed her comment off at the time but went home and cried. I promised myself that I would have lots of shoes one day. Even though we got an employee discount I still could not afford to shop at the Merry Go Round. Most of my stuff came from K-Mart. I now own so many shoes I can't even count them. I have two walk-in closets which are filled to capacity. Not having much back then motivated me to get my life together and have nice things.

Graduating from Governors State, first with my Bachelor Degree and then my master's degree, was a dream come true. It had been a long hard road, but I did it!

My first apartment here in Chicago was a high-rise apartment building on Michigan Avenue with a doorman. It was decorated nicely and I was very proud of it and would always invite people over. It was never a problem if people dropped by uninvited. The last two cars I bought were brand new – no previous owners.

My earlier hardships gave me the motivation to go after the kind of life I originally wanted. Becoming a teen mom did not break me. It made me stronger.

That is why I am so passionate about women living the life of their dreams. It would have been so easy for me to *not* go after my dreams. I could have just let life pass me by. But I never gave up. I hope my story has in some way motivated you. Don't let other people get in your head. You can do whatever you want to do. It may take a little longer, it may be a little harder… But you can do it.

Love always,

Your Big Sis #doingit #dreamlife

Shettima Webb: A Dream Deferred

Harlem

What happens to a dream deferred?
Does it dry up
like a raisin in the sun?
Or fester like a sore—
And then run?
Does it stink like rotten meat?
Or crust and sugar over—
like a syrupy sweet?

Maybe it just sags
like a heavy load.

Or does it explode?

- Langston Hughes

I am usually good at speaking and have no issues talking to people but – for whatever reason – when writing this chapter, I could not formulate the words and put off writing for a million reasons. Perhaps I didn't want to go back to that place that I had locked away and to which I had thrown away the key. A place of shame, a place of hurt, and a place that I had so "conveniently" let go. It's hard to go back to memories of painful times because, often, those times developed in us a defensive mechanism of "convenient forgetfulness." So, in all honesty, some things I have truly forgotten and some things I don't want to say in order to not hurt certain people I love. But my story is my story and it needs to be told.

I reached out to my fellow moms that had already written their stories for this book and they gave me the best advice I could have been given. They told me, "Tell your story. Tell YOUR truth because your truth will help someone else."

So here are my keys as I open the door to my truth.

I grew up on the Westside of Chicago (the Southside ain't got nothing on the Westside, LOL). I was born in the city, 808 N. Lockwood was the address, although we eventually moved to the western suburbs. I was born to two loving but troubled parents. My parents were not drug addicts or alcoholics. They were more the victims of having been too young to marry. My mom was twenty and my dad was twenty-one when they had me. I believe in my heart that they did the very best they could, given their age and lack of life experience. They were married before I was born and are still together to this day but their life was filled with lessons they had to learn on their own and, unfortunately, I had to learn with them. There were lots of arguments both verbal and sometimes physical, so I grew up in an often chaotic home. This in no way is meant to demonize my parents but to merely point out that when you have a baby at a young age – even if you are married – there are certain lessons you and your child are going to go through together.

In my house, I was the counselor. Literally, I would sit on the couch sometimes with both of my parents, or individually, and tell them how they needed to love one another. One might say I grew up fast and I never really enjoyed being a kid because I kind of wasn't one. Growing up in a household as a child who couldn't actually be a child, left me with some emotional scars that I didn't really know I had. Oftentimes, when we give so much of ourselves to people, we lose sight of who we are. And in my case, I had yet to begin to know who I was.

Not only was I dealing with my parents' issues but I had my own issues in school where I was being teased and bullied. I was the chocolate girl with thick hair and back then it was NOT cool to be dark skinned. So, in school, I was left to feel *less than* but at home, I was made to feel *more than* a child. It's funny how that can be perceived as imbalanced but, at the same time, balanced. I can't really remember a time when I ever went to my parents and talked about me. JUST ME. In my mind, my parents had enough going on to deal with personally and I thought, *Why burden them with my problems?* I felt abandoned.

In high school, I was always kind of the loner. I didn't have a bunch of friends, didn't do any extra-curricular activities, and didn't even go to my prom. I was just *there –* except for when I was teased and called ugly. I remember one Valentine's Day when all the girls had candy and balloons from their boyfriends but I didn't. I went into the bathroom and cried because it seemed like every girl in school had a boyfriend but me. Another time, in my freshman year, I saw a cute boy I liked and my friend went to tell him I liked him but he told her I was not his type. What the hell does that mean? I was so hurt and, to be honest, it still bothers me to this day when a man tells me I am not his type. That is truly a sore spot with me. We sometimes don't really ever fully recover from our first hurt but we learn how to not let it hurt as much as it did the first time. That rejection as a freshman, coupled with my parents arguing all the time (not a great example of a healthy relationship), made me not really think about boys.

Then (it may have been in my junior year) my mom noticed all the girls that we went to church with (if you can call it a church, which is another book) were interested in boys and I didn't show any interest at all. One day she said, "All the rest of the girls from church are into boys and you are not. Are you gay?"

This hurt me so bad. *Like, seriously my own mother thinks I am gay at sixteen just because I don't have a boyfriend!?* I snapped back at her, "Like, so you want me to be pregnant like the other girls in school?"

She said, "No."

I said, "I am not gay, never been gay and don't want to be gay."

I was a teenager and with still plenty of time to get a boyfriend. But that question from my mother did something to me. It made me think that if I didn't have a boyfriend people were going to think I was gay. Of course, she didn't mean any harm and later I found out that when she was in school people teased her for being gay because she was not fast, so really she was just concerned I would also get teased. So I get it. Now.

But I didn't get it at age sixteen. Not wanting to look, act or be perceived as gay, I ended up getting in a relationship that I didn't really want to be in. We, as mothers, have to be careful what we say to our children because it can set them on a right or wrong path.

I met my son's father through a friend who told me he had said he liked me. I did not like him at all but my friend convinced me that he was nice, so I gave him a try. I still didn't really like him but he grew on me. Several times I tried to break up with him but he just wouldn't go away. He wasn't a bad person – just not the person for me. I knew this at sixteen but when you don't have the right guidance, sometimes what you really know in your heart does not come out in your actions. I eventually grew to care for him and even love him but I was never *in love* with him. I was a virgin when he and I met and lost my virginity to him. I am not blaming my mother now for my pregnancy but back then I did.

I did not really start having sex until after I had graduated high school. I was eighteen when I asked my mother for birth control pills but she refused to help me get them, thinking to do so would advocate my having sex. You may ask why I didn't go get the birth control pills myself since I was eighteen. The answer is: at the time I felt like I was going against my mom. As a mother, I can understand NOW where she was coming from, but I think if my 18-year-old son told me he was having sex, I would find ways for him *not* to have a baby. But times and ways of thinking have changed. So, because I did not protect myself as I should have, I got pregnant at eighteen and had my son at nineteen.

It was not a happy day for me when I found out I was pregnant. After all, crazy as it sounds, I really didn't want to be with my son's father and now I felt stuck. I felt like I would have to stay with him because we were a family. And I did stay with my son's father, unhappily, for ten years because I didn't want to be judged as being a single mother and because I didn't think anyone else would want me. My advice to young moms is to not stay with your child's father just because he is your child's father. You deserve to be happy and that may not happen with him.

Despite the ups and downs, my parents had in their

own marriage and though they did not approve of my pregnancy, they were very supportive. But even with their support, having low self-esteem and being a teenage mother was
not a great combination. I didn't really believe I was good
enough to be a mother. Oftentimes I felt like I neglected my
son emotionally because I was so caught up in surviving and
providing.

One time, my parents and I got into it over my son
and I left home. That is another chapter perhaps, but I spent
several years being angry at my parents until I learned forgiveness. Forgiveness is an important key to your success.
But don't let anyone rush you or tell you to get over something that has hurt you. You have to forgive in your way and
in your own time.

I worked and went to school because I had to. I beat
myself up because, for a great part of my son's childhood, I
was unhappy, stressed and searching for my own identity.
It's important that I let other mothers know that you can't
beat yourself up for the mistakes you make in your life or
with your children. In addition to me being depressed, my
son had trouble in school. We would constantly argue and
fight about those issues and he eventually had to go to an

alternative school. This set off a whole other set of emotions that I had to deal with. I was constantly blamed for my son being in alternative school and made to feel inadequate as a mother all over again. No one is perfect. My son, who is 17, does not have any babies, does not do drugs and has never been to jail. I did something right.

Not really having a childhood and then having a baby at a young age set off emotions in me of resentment towards my parents and feeling as if my life was over before it had begun. As a young mother, there were many sacrifices that you I had to make (as will you). I suffered from many years of depression. I would work, go to school and come home and get in bed.

PSA ANNOUNCEMENT:

It's important that I stress that I got therapy. Often, especially in the black community, we shun therapy. Therapy was a great decision for me because it provided a voice of reason and support. If you are in need of therapy due to whatever you are going through, please seek help.

Going to school was not easy. I was on welfare and had signed up for the accounting program through what I believe was then called Workforce Development. I remember it was the last day of class and I had to take my finals in order to complete the program. My grandmother had gotten sick and could not keep my son for me so I had to take him with me to the finals. I cried as I got on the bus, off the bus, in class, and when I was ready to go home. I was so embarrassed because I was the only girl in the program that had to have her child at the finals. I remember my teacher encouraging me and telling me she was happy I didn't give up and, no matter what had come in to take the finals. I could have given up and not showed up.

My teacher suggested that I continue the accounting program as my major in college. The hard work I put into going to school paid off because, in 2006, I became the first college graduate in my family with a Bachelor's degree in accounting, business, and finance. And my son was at the graduation.

Before I graduated, I decided to end the 10-year relationship with my son's father. I had gone back and forth with the decision because I knew the importance of maintaining a strong bond between father and son but I was truly unhappy and unfulfilled in the relationship. He and I had gotten into verbal and physical altercations and that was not the life I wanted for my son or myself.

Breaking up with him was a freeing experience and the major step I needed in order to begin the journey of finding out who I was as a person. My son's father did not agree with my decision and over the years we argued back in forth about our son. I do not get along with him nor do I talk to him. Despite our differences, I never kept my son away from his father and they have a good relationship. Unfortunately, sometimes you are not going to get along with your child's father but that does not mean that your child can't have a good relationship with him.

Back in high school, my grandma had paid for me to attend modeling and acting school but because of my parents' finances and my debilitating low self-esteem, I didn't do anything with the modeling and acting certificate. Having a baby deferred my dreams and weight gain put me in the mindset that modeling and acting were not options for me.

During my childhood, I had always been creative. I

loved writing songs, poetry, singing, doing fashion design, and other creative endeavors. Everyone thought I was going to be a fashion designer because I used to rip up my dolls clothes and re-make them. I would create stories and act them out in the mirror. After years of struggling with what I was destined to be and do in life, I opened myself up to try new things.

In 2009, I entered the Miss Illinois Plus America Pageant and won. Then I went on to the nationals where I placed 5th. Juri-Jones Moore was the one who encouraged me to enter the pageant and has been a supporter ever since.

Then I met Chenna Jones, the CEO of the Four Yours Truly Full-Figured Modeling Organization, and we became good friends. I did freelance modeling there for several years. It was through her help and encouragement that I was able to find my love for modeling and eventually make a real career out of it.

Celebrity designer, Glen Duvall of House of Duvall, also encouraged me to continue modeling. These people inspired me and helped me get through some difficult situations in life.

They are the reason I am doing what I love today and each of them helped to kick off my modeling, acting and media career.

I have had the pleasure of interviewing celebrities and traveling to media events as a model and actress. I have modeled for New York Fashion Week, been featured in various magazines, TV, done a national campaign for a pharmaceutical company, and a 3-city tour as an actress. Modeling was the tool God used in order to help me build my self-esteem and put me on a path with purpose.

I started my company, Model Esteem, a modeling and performance arts company that teaches professional modeling with a core focus on anti-bullying lessons and building self-esteem in both youth and adults. Before I was a girl whose dreams had been deferred but somewhere along the way, I decided to become the woman who would not allow past situations hold me back.

Oftentimes, when life happens we give up on our dreams and tell ourselves it was not meant to be. NOT TRUE! Whatever God desires you to be is meant to be even if delayed. I had to forgive my parents, I had to forgive myself. I found my self-worth as a mother and I found my purpose. I no longer feel inadequate as a mother or as a person. You, too, can find your voice and your purpose. You can use your hurt and struggles to empower others. Being a young mother is not easy. There are going to be days when you are ready to give up, but it does get better. Trust me, it gets better! Somewhere someone is waiting for you to give them the keys to your story. So open that door because a dream deferred is still a dream to be accomplished. Go and live your dreams!

Rise Young Girl

Rise young girl.
There are those who will judge for your past,
Those who will never forget your mistakes,
Those who will deem you have lost before the race is finished.

Rise young girl.
When you yourself are broken
And hurts seem too hard to bear,
When your tears are like oceans,

Rise young girl.
You are not what they say you are.
This uneducated lost soul with no hope.
You are what God has destined you to be.

Rise young girl.
Your unspoken words of despair are heard by God.
He has not left you or your child;
Your tears are not in vain.

Rise young girl.
Life to you might seem like death
And you feel like there is nothing left to give.
But there is purpose in you to give to this world.

Rise young girl.
Because even the Savior in all his glorious works had to be res-
urrected,
So rise young girl, rise;
Go forth and save others
To help them Rise.

-Shettima Webb
Inspired by Maya Angelou

161

Melanie Foote-Davis: Don't Drop Your Baby

I am so glad you're here. The fact that you're reading this says to me that you have a vested interest in you and your baby's future. That makes me extremely proud of you.

Let's keep it real. The path that you are on is not going to be easy. It is not a cake walk. There will be days when you'll feel like giving up. Some of your friends and family may say or do things that will cause you to feel ashamed, guilty or unworthy for getting pregnant and having your baby.

I remember missing a party because my daughter was sick. I wanted my friend to be supportive and understanding but she wasn't. Instead, she said, "You could have fun if you didn't have a baby." I was fine with missing the party. I was concerned about my child but her words still hurt my feelings. I also used to get threatening phone calls. They said they would f**k a pregnant girl up. They threatened to kick my a** at school. We didn't have Caller I.D in 1983. So I didn't know who was calling me. I didn't know who to trust. I didn't know who had my back or who would stab me in my back. Although I knew my family was there for me. Sometimes I felt very alone. You may feel alone sometimes. I want you to know that you are not alone. I've been there. Don't give up. You are worthy. Your baby is blessed to have you. The ability to bring life into the world is a beautiful gift.

Like many teen girls, I was searching for my identity. I spent a great deal of my childhood trying to accept my differences. I was a young girl with strong family ties and tremendous potential. I was blessed with a father who was a great provider and a nurturing mother who created space for me to have my own thoughts and opinions.

Yet, I had a hard time figuring out what it meant to be me. Where should I have gone to find the answer to who I was when life seemed so complicated to me? My hormones were raging. Everything on the outside looked good, but inside I felt lost and lonely.

In my mind, everything about me was different from the way I looked to the way I felt. I thought differently. I liked peace. They liked gossip. I didn't like living in the country. I dreamed of living somewhere more progressive. I wanted to live in a place where no one laughed at you for speaking grammatically correct. Where I'm from, they laughed at you for that. My older siblings lived about an hour away in Washington, DC and I used to get away to the city as much as possible. I spent a lot of weekends and most of my summers there with my sisters. That was my escape. I felt happy and free there.

At home, I felt disconnected. I didn't like being smart because it made me stand out from the people I wanted to connect with. I wanted to fit in. I wanted to belong somewhere. So I experimented and did things that would not make my mother proud. I started drinking, smoking cigarettes and weed. Why? Because I wanted to blend, yet I never did. It never felt right.

I learned later that I was asking the wrong question. The question wasn't, "How do I fit in?" The question was, "What will it take for me to accept who I am?" I wanted to be heard, valued and accepted for being me. Trying to please others and conform to what I thought they wanted was exhausting. Whew! I'm tired now just thinking about it.

You hear things like, "Act like a lady." What does that mean to you? Does it mean you just need to be pretty and not smart? Does it mean you need to cook, clean and have babies? Does it mean you must dress a certain way to get a boy to like you? Does it mean that you can't be a high achiever? Does it mean that you're too aggressive if you find your voice, set clear boundaries and have an opinion of your own?

Why can't we be comfortable with what feels right and natural for us? We get stuck on gender roles and box our girls in. Maybe you prefer pants over dresses, like football and not cheerleading, prefer ponytail over curls. Maybe you're not pink and purple and don't like princess movies. Maybe you don't want to be pretty in pink. Maybe you feel pretty in print. It doesn't make you less of a girl or a lady. It makes you, you.

Blending never felt right to me because I was not born to blend. Blending would mean standing in the shadows of someone else's light. I was created to stand in my own light. You were meant to stand in your own light as well.

It is harder now. Your generation is inundated with technology –technology that has essentially placed you in a difficult situation. You are exposed to more than you even realize. You spend a huge portion of your day in front of some type of screen like televisions, smart phones, tablets, and computers. Technology has given you access to a world

Did you know that images carry messages? These messages are encouraging you to buy into concepts that objectify you as a woman. These messages are taking your power away. They are telling you that you would be better if you were a duplicate of someone else. It's possibly breaking your spirit because it's swallowing up the essence of who you are. You may not even realize it.

These images and messages are telling you who you should be, how you should behave and what you should look like. Images include things like billboards, videos, reality-television and magazine ads. Paying too much attention to these images, what's happening on social media, and listening to other people's opinions of you, can cause you to question who you are.

You may begin to compare yourself to others and wish for what they have. Comparing yourself to others can be harmful to your self-esteem. You give your power away when your mind begins to wander and think things like:

- I wish I had Beyoncé's body.
- I wish I had more followers online.

167

- I'm not pretty enough.
- I'm not smart enough.
- I wish I were cool instead of smart.
- I wish I were popular and could fit in.

Are you secretly wishing your friends could see you for who you are? That's what happens when you try to fit into the images on the screens. In the midst of all of that, your dreams, your joy, and your self-worth are trapped inside this screen trying to get out. You are suffocating all the beauty of who you are.

This is why it is important for you to stay connected to God and get in touch with yourself. When others make you question who you are based on what someone else is doing, it's like saying God failed when he made you.

That is absolutely not true. How dare they insult God by leading you to believe that he made a mistake when he created you? It's time to stop the madness and break free from the box that society is keeping you in. You have another person who is counting on you to shine.

Today is your day to say, "Yes!" to the loving, the amazing woman you are becoming. You have everything you need. You are not a mistake. Your baby is not a mistake. Sweetheart, you are a gift to this world. All you need to do is believe it. Accept that.

"Be YOU! The world will adjust."

-Unknown

Don't spend your time wishing for something someone else has. Instead look for the things that you can celebrate within you. It is time to stand in your greatness and BE YOU WITHOUT APOLOGY! It is a waste of your time and energy trying to be a carbon copy of someone else. As Sweet Brown would say, "Ain't nobody got time for that!" You've got a beautiful baby waiting on you to write your own story. You are the only one who can tell your story. You are the only one who can live your dream. You are the only one who can live out your purpose. There is no one who can live your life and walk in your shoes the way that you can.

My parents were older than my peers' parents. They were born in the 1920's. Some of the old-school thinking was a part of my upbringing. One day I gathered the courage to ask my mother about birth control. If I tell you that I was raised in the church, I bet you can guess what she told me. You're right. She said to save myself for marriage. I thought, Marriage? You must be kidding me. Why would I want to be married when I didn't see many happy marriages around me?

No one was having the conversation that I really needed. No one was talking to me about body safety. No one was teaching me how to manage my desire to belong. People weren't telling me how to manage the crush I had with boys. They told me to remain a virgin. They never talked to me about condom negotiation or how to have safer sex if and when I found myself in a compromising situation. Let's face it, talking about sexual health is uncomfortable for a lot of people. I know that my family meant well and did the best they could. They could only teach me what they knew.

So I created my own sense of independence. I decided to explore on my own. I dated an older guy. He was more experienced than me. I was curious about the very thing everyone told me not to do. I read books and magazines. Again, I felt alone. So I explored.

I am sharing this with you simply to show you that I am no better than you. I didn't always do the right thing. My choices led me to a very scary situation.

Truth moment: Becoming a teenage mother was not my dream. I wanted a daughter, but not as a teen. Yet there I was fitting into a few statistical categories. I was a teenage girl. I was single. I was black. I was pregnant. Now, what? According to societal expectations, I was going to be a high school drop-out on welfare. I was going to have a few more kids by different baby daddies within a few short years.

Life is about perspective. It's all in the way you look at things, including the way you look at yourself. I didn't see myself the way that others did. That is definitely not how I saw my child. Absolutely not! My daughter Trinity was not a mistake. She is a beautiful, unexpected blessing. I feel honored that God entrusted me to carry her in my womb. I see her as my most treasured gift.

They were wrong. I finished high school and continued on to became a licensed cosmetologist by the time I was eighteen. I continue to seek knowledge daily. I am a best-selling author and I enjoy doing what I love as my own boss.

Trinity was my first and only pregnancy. I had whispered secrets to her as an infant and they were true. She is incredible. She graduated from the prestigious Spelman College. She has a master's degree in economics. She experiences various cultures through global travel and a diverse network. She approaches life with courage and adventure. I couldn't be more proud of the phenomenal woman she has grown into. My eyes water as I type this. Can you feel my pride?

Life is also about choices. I made the choice to have unprotected sex. It wasn't a safe choice. But I can't go back and change that now. I had to face my reality and decide where I was going from there. Something deep inside of me knew that my life would be great. I know that your life will be great, also. Your life is your story. You have the power to create the story you want to tell. You get to choose how your story will end. Start with choosing to believe in yourself. Believe that you have value and your life matters. Stop. Say these aloud.

"My life matters."

"My life has meaning and purpose."

"I am worthy of a great life."

"I am creating an amazing life for me and for my baby."

Choose to believe that you have purpose. There are many who live in the perspective of, "Your Life is ruined," because they chose to have a child. That's a lie! It's not over unless you say it is. Having a baby may have delayed the process and changed the course of your path. It did not change your destiny.

I know that you handle your child with care. You coddle your baby gently to make sure that you don't drop her or him. You nurture your baby by making sure that she or he is fed, clothed and clean. Your goal is to protect your child and keep her or him safe and healthy. Like me, you want the best for your baby. If you tripped, you would instinctively hold your baby tightly. You might hurt yourself but you would never drop your child.

Having had a baby means that you chose to give life to a beautiful being. I'm counting on you to do just that, to continue to give life. What do I mean by that? I mean that it is important for you to remember that you are capable of giving birth. That means you can also birth dreams. I said all of that to emphasize this. You had a baby inside of you when you were born. That baby is your purpose, your dreams, and your goals. Now you have two babies. The baby you carried for nine months and the dream that you have inside. Don't drop your babies.

I encourage you to hold on to your dream baby in the same way that you hold on to your physical baby. Your dreams don't have to die because you're a teen mom.

Let's take a moment to reflect. What did you dream of doing or becoming before you were pregnant?

_____

_____

_____

Guess what? You can still live your dream. You can give life to your goals and your dreams. Think about how pursuing your dreams will create a great life for you and your baby.

_____

Here are a few simple steps for you to follow:

4. Identify your goal or dream.

5. Believe that it is possible for you, regardless of the opinions of others.

6. Make the decision. Say, "Yes!" to going for it with all you have.

7. Determine what actions you need to take to achieve your goal.

8. Ask for help. Who can help you? (Examples include: family, counselor, mentor)

9. Surround yourself with people who believe in you.

10. Take actions every day that lead you closer to your dreams.

11. Celebrate every accomplishment no matter how small you think it is.

I'm not going to pretend that it is going to be easy. See your child as worthy of your best. See yourself as a phenomenal woman, worthy of the best no matter how hard it gets. You don't have to do this alone. Pride will stand in the way of your dreams if you let it. Release your pride. Remain open to receiving help when someone offers it. Have the courage to ask for help. Asking for help does not make you weak. It is actually a sign of strength, courage, and wisdom. We all need a village, including you. None of us got where we are without help from someone else. I had family and friends that supported me the entire time. I am not ashamed of that. I am grateful for their love and support.

There are a few more things I want to share with you before I go. These are incredibly important in helping you to nurture both your human baby and your dream. Children are gifts. So what if your baby wasn't planned? Know that your life and your babies' lives have purpose and value. Guide, nurture, encourage, teach, protect and treat them as your most precious treasure.

Prioritize. Make decisions based on what will be in the best interest of your children and you. It is going to require sacrifice and compromise. Remember, you don't have to do this alone.

It is important for you to take a stand to protect your children. Children are impressionable. You must be aware of everything you say and do in front of them. Take a look at your environment and your behaviors. Be willing to let go of behaviors that are not taking you to where you want to go. These behaviors include the way you live, who you hang out with and the conversations that you have. There may be people in your life that you must release as well. Let's look at your relationships.

Who do you expose your child to? Who do you and your baby spend time with?

_____

_____

_____

What do you and your friends spend time doing?

_____

_____

_____

Are these activities helping you get to where you want to go? Yes or No

Are you comfortable talking about your dreams with the friends that you have? Yes or No

Do the people you hang out with encourage you when you talk about your dreams? Yes or No

You are on the right track if you answered, "Yes," to these questions. However, if you answered, "No," to any of these questions, it is decision time. It is time for you to let some people go. I know that the thought of keeping a safe distance from friends that you've known a long time may feel hard. I encourage you to see beyond this moment. Pause. Take a deep breath. Think about how your choices will impact your future. Your child does not need to meet every person that you know.

Are you willing to let go of toxic relationships for the sake of creating a great life for your baby? Yes or No

You are a living example of what you want for your children. They will watch everything you do. They will hear everything you say to them or around them. You are their first role model. What do they see, hear or experience by watching you? Words have power. We begin to believe what we continue to hear and say. Pay attention to what you say to your children. Choose your words carefully. Pay attention to what others say around them too. Speak life into their future by using words of encouragement.

As I mentioned earlier, I used to sit in my room talking to my Trinity as I held her. She was the sweetest and most adorable being I had ever met. I used to kiss her forehead and tell her how much I loved her. I told her how important she was to me. I told her that she was beautiful and smart. I told her that she was brilliant. I told her that she was the best gift I ever received. I remember how she looked at me. She was only a newborn baby, but she looked at me like she truly understood. I was speaking positivity and love into her life. That gave me a sense of peace.

I realized something by the time Trinity was two and half years old. I realized that I loved her father but I wasn't *in love* with him. I realized that I was only in a relationship with him because he was the father of my baby and my family liked him. I wanted my daughter to have two parents like I did. But I wasn't happy. I don't believe that he was happy either. I couldn't see a future with him. Staying in a relationship out of obligation was not healthy. It wasn't fair to me to stay. It wasn't fair to him to ask him to stay in a relationship he didn't want either. I believed that my daughter could have both parents without us having to be a couple. So I broke up with him.

We agreed that he would spend time with her every other weekend. That lasted for a month or so. Then she told me that she didn't want to go to his house. I asked her why. She said that she wasn't with him. He dropped her off with his grandmother or with her godfather's girlfriend. So I told her she didn't have to go. I called him to tell him not to pick her up that weekend. I explained why. He said ok. He rarely called to check on her or pick her up after that. I later discovered that he was beginning to use drugs. I didn't want her in that environment, anyway. So I didn't reach out to him either. I would rather her be safe even if that meant not being around her father. Her safety was my priority.

Here's the thing. Remember when I said to be careful of what you say to or around your children? This is what I want you to know: I did not fill Trinity's head with negative talk about her father.

I admit that I was angry and disappointed in him for abandoning his daughter. Once I was so furious that I drove for hours with a baseball bat in the car. I wanted to beat his head in for abandoning my child. Every time I reached a destination, I was told that he had just left. It was nothing but the grace of God that saved him. Now, I am glad God intervened.

After the fury subsided, I decided that whatever relationship she developed with him would just happen organically. I wouldn't want to force my anger or thoughts about him on her. Are you following me? I did not speak of him badly in her presence. She didn't hear me call him names or say things like, "your no-good father." That was not healthy for her. It wasn't healthy for me either. It was not the best use of my words nor was it the best use of my time. Whatever feelings she now has about him are not influenced by me or my words.

I knew that we would be fine with or without him. I did not drop my baby. We moved on in spite of our situation. Our life didn't stop because of that. So remember to speak life into your child. Focus on the things you want, not what you don't want. Guard your children's environment against others who will feed their minds with toxic information.

My goal was for us to co-parent. I wanted us to raise her together without being together as a couple. That did not happen because of *his* choices, not mine. I have no power over someone else's choices and neither do you. We can only control our own. I strongly believe that children can be raised in a healthy way when parents work together even if they are not together as a couple. You may get angry with the father of your baby at times. He may disappoint you. Remember that all of your choices have an impact on your child. Be very careful. Keep your environment healthy for the sake of your baby. Choose your words carefully in the presence of your child. Also remember that your baby is a little human being with feelings and emotions – not a pawn. Please don't use your child as a bargaining tool to get what you want or to get revenge on their father if he hurts you. Talk your disagreements out privately to avoid your baby growing up feeling like her or his father is the source of your problems. Don't drop your baby. Your baby has feelings too. Do what's best for your baby, not what's best for your emotions in the moment.

Spend quality time with your children. Make them feel important. *Cherish* each moment with them. Choose quality time over material things. Great moments last a lifetime. Your children will remember what you did with them longer than they will remember what you bought them.

Learn to love yourself. Taking care of you is one of the best gifts you can give to your baby. There are going to be days when you want to give up and feel like you are losing your mind. Take time to exhale and do something that brings you joy and peace, things that are healthy for you and your family. The best way for you to give something good to your child is by giving to yourself. Love *you* by treating yourself kindly, eating well, feeding your mind with positive things and surrounding yourself with people who empower you and help you grow.

Here are a few tips to help you take care of you. We're more vulnerable when we are emotional. Make decisions based on wisdom, not emotions. There is power in a pause. Pause, exhale and think before taking action. A few seconds can literally save your life.

Things to remember:

Your child's best interest: Be mindful of your environment.

- Becoming more aware of what is present in your thinking affords you the opportunity to clearly see your options

- Create healthy boundaries and make healthier choices.

Create your village

- Find yourself a mentor.
- Find mentors for your children. Put them in enrichment programs.
- Choose your friends carefully. Hang out with dream makers.
- Say, "Good-bye," to dream stealers and dream breakers.

Speak Life. Your words have power.

- Believe in yourself.
- See the possibility, not the obstacle.
- Speak life and possibility into your desired situation.

Love *You.*

- God created you to be brilliant, purposeful and beautiful.
- Accept who you are.
- Take time to breathe.
- Ask for help (I can't stress that enough).

Don't Drop Your Baby!

- Nurture your child with love, time, encouragement, guidance and attention.
- Nurture your dreams like a baby that needs love and attention.
- Take steps every day that lead you to where you want to go.

Celebrate your journey. Stop now to celebrate you.

- You are here because you have taken steps towards a brighter future. Celebrate that.
- No matter how small, acknowledge your accomplishments.
- Acknowledge your children's accomplishments as well.

Know that I believe in you and that your life doesn't end here. Don't drop your baby! As long as you have breath, you still have purpose. Dream BIG! Go Forth and Conquer!

I would love to hear how things are going for you.

Millionaire M.O.M. Challenge #3

"You gain strength, courage, and confi-
dence by every experience in which you really
stop to look fear in the face...You must do the
thing you think you cannot do."

-Eleanor Roosevelt

Your dreams are worth fighting for. A lot of the time, fighting for our dreams will require us to move in spite of fear. For the next seven days, do one thing every day that scares you. Start the business. Write the book. Apply for the job. Submit your admission application. Do whatever it is that you have been putting off because of fear.

Reflect on the following questions:

1. How did it feel to conquer your fear?
2. What did you learn from the experience?
3. What fear will you conquer next?

IV. I RELEASE MY PAST AND EMBRACE MY PROMISE

"The knowledge of the past stays with us. To let go is to release the images and emotions, the grudges and fears, the clinging and disappointments of the past that bind our spirits."

— *Jack Kornfield*

I am not a hostage of my past. I forgive those who have wronged me. I forgive myself for my past decisions and actions. I am exactly where I am supposed to be in life. My future begins now, and I live for it and all of the promise it holds for me.

Dr. Catrina Pullum: Labels

Who is Dr. Trina Pullum? Who was I supposed to be? Who have I become? Why is any of this important to you?

It is important to you because my story could be yours. You might draw a number of parallels between my life and your own once you read my story. That is why my story is so important because it shows that no matter the hand you're dealt in life, no matter what label people place on you, you can overcome and become whatever God has destined for your life. Over the years, I have worn many labels. Wife. Mother. Servant. Manager. Counselor. Life Coach. Educator. Mentor. Advocate. While any of these titles could describe me, when it comes to my life story, one word stands out above them all. Survivor!

I am a native of New Orleans and consider both Texas and Louisiana my homes. I am currently married and raising four children ranging from ages of twenty-three down to nine.

My beginning

I am the product of teen parents and I myself became a teen mother. That component of what statistics report does hold some truth but that is where the truth starts and ends for me. Though I am the product of teen parents, I was reared by adults that were much more mature. Those that contributed to my upbringing were my great grandmother, grandparents, and uncles. I found myself growing up with my uncles being, in a sense, my brothers. My parents later established other relationships separate from one another, yet my mother and step-father remained an active force and support system in my life. The adults in my life insured that I receive a sound education and established a relationship with God. Attending church in my family was not an option but a mandate because I was born into a family of pastors and active church leaders. This meant I grew up in ministry and was always actively involved in some way. I've had the privilege of serving as an International Youth Pastor, Women Ministry Leader and Praise Team Leader. I attribute my life's journey and the accomplishments thereof to the support of the family God blessed me with and ultimately to God and the favor that he's shown me.

My story

I am the daughter of a teen mother. Some would have labeled me as lost just because of being the product of my birth. My great-grandmother took me into her home to raise me. Although my mother wanted to raise me, she decided to move in with someone who was not my biological father. My great-grandmother did not like that situation and asked my mother to let me live within her home. My mother agreed.

I formed my initial view of the world through my elders' eyes. The heart and mind of my great-grandmother laid a foundation which gave me something to build on as I went through life. I grew up in the church, drawing joy, laughter, and light from that refuge. Yet, some of my first and greatest pains started in the church as well. I was subjected to abuse at an early age by a trusted member of my church family. It was devastating.

I also grew up longing for the presence of my father in my life. When my natural parents decided to marry other people, they drew lines in the sand that relationships struggled to cross. My family gave me great support, but could not fill all the voids that appeared in my life.

The pain of the early abuse translated into new labels for me, the primary label being, silent! I felt unable to tell anyone about what happened to me. Being unable to express the pain outwardly, I was determined to numb it. This gave birth to the next label in my life, alcoholic. By the time I was twelve years old, I began drinking on a regular basis and hid it from my family (since I was under age). As with all things done in the dark, they eventually come to light.

My behavior changed and my great-grandmother, unable to explain or correct it, decided it was time for me to live with my grandmother. My alcohol dependence came to my family's attention. They intervened, and although they never got to the original root problem, they did help me stop using alcohol to dull my pain.

I grew into a beautiful young woman, and while I was very focused on school, I still sought that older male attention I felt was missing. My first experiences with the opposite sex lead to a new label, mother. To the outside observer, it would seem that the cycle continued unbroken, teen mothers begetting teen mothers. Although my life embarked on a new and unexpected path, I resolved that my goals and dreams would remain unfettered.

Giving birth to my son at age seventeen, I still completed high school and went on to college. While in college, I experienced more of the life lessons that come with age as my great-grandmother's health deteriorated. Going to school, raising a young son, and helping to care for an aging adult parent – to say I was stretched thin would be an understatement. I wanted to quit or give up so many times. Instead, I gave my best to every endeavor I engaged in. I achieved. I excelled. However, my tests and trials were not over, in fact, they were just beginning.

I got involved with someone who seemed to be the perfect man. Given the pressures of living at home, after a whirlwind romance, I moved in with my love. I soon found that the light of love I thought I was entering into was a darker, grim place, with much more pain. I soon found myself under the thumb of an abusive man. I was sexually assaulted, regularly beaten, choked unconscious, and ultimately held at knifepoint. A new label was created in my life, domestic abuse survivor.

I prayed to God to get me out of the situation and when push came to shove, I left. During this time, my great-grandmother passed away. She was the first mother I had really known. When you think life cannot get worse, it seems to always find a way to do so. Between the loss of my great-grandmother and the abuse I suffered at the hands of my boyfriend, I found myself in great pain. But I had a vision.

I knew the vision my great-grandmother had for my life. I understood the vision and the plan that God had for my life. Both helped me form my own vision for my life which allowed me to see I had to rise above the situation I was in.

Because of my vision, I managed to overcome the hurt and pain of this situation, graduate college, and move away from my abuser for a fresh start in my life.

I kept the faith, drive, and fortitude that had brought me thus far and it kept growing. I took on several expanding roles through different companies. I earned my MBA, leading me to management and leadership roles where I worked. I moved into the public sector, working as an advocate for children and as a forensic investigator. I watched my child grow into a smart and stable young man. I grew in my ministry which lead to my Honorary Doctorate of Divinity degree.

Growing up as the product of teen parents and then becoming a teen parent myself, I have experienced firsthand the challenges of growing up in difficult circumstances. However, through faith, along with the guidance of my grandparents and extended family, I beat the odds. I have used those experiences to fuel my passion as a tireless advocate for abused children and women serving my community in a variety of roles.

My testimony

The statistics weigh in against teen mothers. Like many issues of today, teen pregnancy tends to run in cycles. Teen mothers beget more teen parents, mainly because they have not had the time to grow up themselves. According to the statistics, teenage mothers are less likely to complete high school and are more likely to end up on welfare (nearly 80% of unmarried teen mothers end up on welfare). Additionally, the children of teen parents are more likely to perform poorly in school and are at greater risk of abuse and neglect. The sons of teen mothers are 13% more likely to end

up in prison while teen daughters are 22% more likely to become teen mothers themselves.

Though this may be true, I thank God that *man* did
not write my story. My story has played out far differently
from what statistics show. It all depends on whose report you
believe. Having faith in a higher power, having a functional
and helpful support system, and an understanding of your
purpose and direction in maintaining your focus when times
are rough are the keys that got me through my journey.

That is not to say my journey has even been *close* to
easy. My journey from trial to triumph has been challenging
and at times rather difficult. However, it has been very inter-
esting. For every lesson, there has been a blessing. The abuse
I suffered at a young age caused pain and scars that I did not
and could not share with anyone. I thought I was alone. I was
hurt and in a place where I felt that I should have been the
safest. Knowing what I know now, I wish I had told someone
what was going on. I wish I had shared the pain I was feeling,
instead of internalizing it. I was young and it was not my
fault; I know that now. If you are going through such a difficulty now, talk to someone you trust. Also, listen carefully
to the children around you. Pay attention, get a baseline of

their behavior, and then watch for differences.

I became a mother during my senior year of high school at the age seventeen so, as I was finishing school, I had already started my journey to becoming a single mother. Being a mother poses its own set of complexities, but being a single teenage mother causes those challenges to double. This is where my support system came in. I hope that you can find that support system within your family. Your vision will change. Things you planned and dreamed for your life will change. I was supposed to go to Spellman College. I no longer had a social life because I had a child. When I did things for school, my family was there supporting me and helping me take care of my son but the extras--the fun stuff--I was on my own for those. My suggestion to you is to write down your vision for your life and share it with your supporters. Knowing they are supporting a future for you and your child can make a difference in their level of support. If you cannot find it in your family, find it in close friends. Make sure that you live up to your vision. Put the plan into motion and see it through. I am eternally grateful for the support and love of my family and the favor of God all of which have allowed me to overcome many challenges that would have consumed most. My family taught me how to become a parent and then made sure that I completed high school on time.

I am proud to say that I completed high school with honors and went on to further my education, something that "they" say does not happen for teen mothers. I initially earned a Bachelor of Science degree in Psychology and Criminal Justice. I later pursued and earned an Executive M.B.A. in Healthcare Management and a Clinical master's degree in Social Work with a specialization in Disaster Mental Health. I earned my Master Certification in Forensic Psychology, Nonprofit Management as well as a Doctorate in Divinity. I have also earned several other certifications. You can do anything you put your mind to! Decide what you want for your life and your family. Determine what God has purposed in your life and you will succeed. The road God ordained for me has not been traveled with ease, however, with God, family, self-determination, motivation and the desire to succeed, I've been able to accomplish that which others have said could not be done.

I am currently married with four children. Though my oldest was the product of a single teen mother, he too has defeated the odds. He graduated high school at the age of sixteen, is pursuing his first college degree and owns his own entertainment company. My other children are still in school and all are positively engaged in different activities in pursuit of their success. I must say that my hard work and many sacrifices have paid off – not only for myself and my family but for all the youth and families I've had the privilege of servicing. My calling is not to arrive at a static destination, but to travel a pathway to constant growth and transformation. I want to encourage you to see the opportunity for growth and transition when things in your life become difficult – for this will help you become stronger and wiser just as the Bible teaches that trials come to make us strong. I incite, motivate, and encourage those entrusted to my care to live a fulfilling life! I continue to demonstrate a passion and fire for advocating on behalf of victims of child abuse and domestic violence– especially teens, college students and young mothers. Helping survivors of D.V. is one of my passions because I myself am a survivor of that situation.

As I mentioned earlier, during my senior year of college, I became a victim of domestic violence. This relationship terminated quickly when my ex-boyfriend placed a knife to my throat. I had no one to educate me as to how to deal with domestic violence. Being a Criminal Justice major and working in the legal system, the only thing I knew was the legal side of putting my abuser in jail. I speak not just from gained knowledge, but from personal experience.

What I have accomplished – so far

My transparency makes me very effective in the work I do. I am the President of RARE, Inc., an organization committed to the personal development of young women, in which I have served as a mentor for young women who have experienced trauma through sexual assault and/or domestic violence. I am dedicated to training young women by using practical and biblical principles empowering them to live a fulfilled and enriched life. My God-given talent/gift is to empower lives and heal hearts!

In the summer of 2013, I added "co-author" to my growing list of titles with the release of *It Takes A Village To Raise A Child: An Afrocentric Approach.* I also co-authored, *Confessions of a Domestic Violence Survivor*, which was released in October 2013. In 2014, my book *Breaking the Chains: From Hurting to Healing* was published. It tells more of my story and how I used the pain in my life to arrive at my life's purpose.

I have been recognized for my life's work with accolades from the Louisiana House of Representatives, the Mayor of McKinney, TX and the Baton Rouge Office of Mayor-President and have received numerous other awards from business, religious and community groups.

So the moral, if you will, to my story is simple…do not let others label you. The only labels you need recognize or respond to are the labels God gives to you, no one else's.

Sylvia Duncan: Don't Let It Stop You

*"Every great dream begins with a
dreamer."*

-Anonymous

He lived across the street from our new home. He had a big afro and a smile like Jermaine Jackson of The Jackson Five. After we moved in, sometimes I would sit at the window in our living room and watch as he and his sisters played in their front yard or when he mowed the lawn. I was captivated by him. His family seemed so normal, like how I would view a white family to be at that time. His mom and the man I would later learn was his step-dad seemed very happy with each other – the perfect couple. I could almost sense that what was going on in our house couldn't possibly be going on in his house. Thinking about him helped me to escape the reality of what was going on in my own home.

His name was Clinton. He was one of eight siblings. Before **It** happened, Dad saw that this boy was showing interest in me and he would say to me, "You don't have time for that, keep your mind on school." By "that," he meant boys. He was right; besides, the truth was that although I was a little smitten by Clinton, I really didn't want a boyfriend. I always imagined that there was more to life and I wanted it. I wanted a life much different from the life I was living at that time.

When we lived in our small apartment in the Stateway Gardens housing project, fear and anxiety ruled. As a young girl, I would spend my time dreaming of who I would be when I grew up and boys weren't part of those dreams. So, although I was infatuated with Clinton, I knew my feelings of infatuation wouldn't last; I was focused.

For that matter, I had very few friends. It wasn't that I didn't want to make friends in our new community, I just didn't want people to know what was going on inside the walls of our new home. I was ashamed of the violence that my siblings and I witnessed on what seemed like a regular basis. So, I kept my distance and I kept my dreams.

We had not lived in our new home for 6 months before **It** happened. **It** was the thing that changed my life; the violence I had experienced in my home came to an end. My mother shot and killed my father. I was a sophomore in high school. Once **It** happened, everything changed. I was no longer the little girl who believed there was more to life, and Clinton was no longer someone I occasionally watched from our living room window.

He began visiting me often after the tragedy – first, sitting in the same living room I watched him from, then staying overnight. After **It** happened, it seemed, just like that, I lost my focus. The future I once imagined for myself seemed more like make-believe than a possible reality.

If **It** hadn't happened, things would have been different. Dad would never have allowed a boy to stay overnight in our home. But, there Clinton was, in the place where I would often sit and think about my future; my room. For years, despite the violent reality in our small apartment in Stateway Gardens, I had dreamed that things could be better for me, for my siblings, and for my family. In an instant, everything I wanted for myself, for my future, my dreams and aspirations were all gone.

Our lives were turned upside down. And though we were no longer on pins and needles wondering if there would be violence in our home, we were still on edge with every appearance in court to find out our mothers' fate. Each court date had us anxiously wondering if that day was the day she would be taken away from us. To tell you the truth, Mom wasn't really emotionally present for quite a while after **It** happened and neither were we, for that matter. We all seemed to go our separate ways. Though we lived in the same house, we became familiar strangers. Mom cried all the time. The truth is that, regardless of what happened, she had loved Dad.

I can still recall the moment the doctor said I was pregnant. My heart dropped, tears filled my eyes and questions filled my head. How could I let this happen? Pregnant? How would I, or could I, tell my mother? What would my siblings think of me? If he were here, what would Dad think? I felt alone and afraid. After we received the news, Clinton never really looked at me the same.

He didn't want a child and he found all kinds of ways of making me aware of that fact, including dating someone else. If I had known he would turn out to be the person he became in that moment, I would never have allowed our relationship to become intimate. Now, looking back, I see that I was only drawn to Clinton because he represented something I longed for…a normal family life and when Dad was gone, something I missed…a father figure. I didn't act wildly promiscuous, but the progression of my relationship with Clinton, made me question myself. But it was too late.

I was pregnant. Blaming myself (or him, for that matter), wasn't going to change what was now my reality. In my mind, whatever I thought I wanted while growing up, had just been erased with two words…you're pregnant. Mom wasn't happy when I finally told her, she didn't say anything, but I could tell she was disappointed.

It was so draining for me to attend court while pregnant. Deep inside, I hoped the judge would see that Mom had a pregnant daughter and show compassion, but that never happened. Each time we entered the courtroom, I visibly trembled with fear. It took everything in me just to walk to the section where we sat with our uncle, behind Mom and her attorney. The level of anxiety was unreal. Every time a continuance was ordered by the Judge, our sighs of relief would be short-lived. Even though we physically walked out of the courtroom with our mother, emotionally we left pieces of ourselves on our bench in the section behind where Mom sat with her attorney, to hold our place until we returned.

Eventually, Mom was found guilty and had to go to prison. Because of appeals and a new attorney, her time spent there was not so much time that my siblings and I would never see her again but it was enough time that we found ourselves literally caring for ourselves for months at a time. We were careful to keep ourselves off the Department of Children Services' radar by going to school and doing all the normal things we did before Mom went away. However, with no parental guidance, we also did things that weren't so normal.

Soon after Mom went away, I gave birth to a son. Life became even more difficult for me. I struggled to finish high school but often missed classes due to illness, my son's and mine. Morning sickness or doctors' appointments had become a normal part of my life. And, what was more trying than being pregnant, was enduring the constant whispers from classmates as I walked down the halls. It was disturbing how unkind my classmates had become. I often thought I would rather bear the violence I witnessed in my childhood than hear the snide, hurtful remarks from classmates. Some days, I would be so distraught that it would take me hours to dress for school. I barely passed all my senior classes and I debated whether to attend graduation. I didn't think I could handle the harsh looks and unkind comments. Besides, neither of my parents would be there. So for me, there really was no reason to attend graduation.

That is until one of my classmates, who hadn't joined in on the cruelty, convinced me to go by saying, "It doesn't matter that you've had a child. That shouldn't change anything you wanted for yourself. Your life doesn't have to end. Besides, your parents would want you to go."

She was right. Having a child, should not have changed what I desired for myself. Sure, if I could have gone back in time to that moment, I would have made different decisions. I would have remembered Dad's words saying, "You don't have time for that, keep your mind on school." And I would have done just that – kept my mind on school.

But, I couldn't go back. I could only find a way to go forward. And. Although life before **It** was life-changing in itself, my parents did the best they could with what they had. With all their faults, they loved me and my siblings. They would have wanted me to attend my high school graduation. When my best friend's Mom said she would attend on behalf of my Mom, I felt better – and with that, decided to go. It made me realize that yes, life with a child was going to be a little tougher, but it would not be impossible. That revelation was...

The Turning Point for My Life

After graduation, I decided to get a job rather than attend college. I reasoned that college would require money and take time. I didn't see how I could attend college and care for a child. I really wanted to go on to college but, frankly, with my final high school grades, I didn't think I could or would be accepted into a higher institution of learning.

The only guidance I received from my high school guidance counselor was vague and mixed with prying inquiries about the tragedy that happened in my home. She seemed more interested in bringing up my pain than assisting me with college applications. Although my friend had encouraged me to attend graduation, she couldn't show me what to do next and though I had been excited to walk across the stage and receive a diploma, I felt I had earned it simply because I endured the cruelty of classmates – not because of my grades. So the excitement of graduating quickly waned when faced with reality and it made sense to forget about college and just get a job. It's strange how easy it came to me to reconcile my dream for what I wanted to do with my life with planning a future with a baby. Before my pregnancy, choosing between college and something else would have been a "no-brainer." Of course, college would have been the choice. But choosing between college and feeding your child, that's a different story – feeding your child was the "no brainer." I needed an income.

I had very little job experience, poor high school grades, and no idea where to start. During my senior year, I had attempted to work at a local sandwich shop. The hours were impossible, I had to leave school and go directly to the restaurant. After my shift ended at 11pm, I had to take a one-hour bus ride home arriving to uncompleted homework and, oftentimes, a screaming child. I worked at that restaurant for less than three weeks before I decided to quit. The pay wasn't enough to cover the round trip bus fare to school and barely covered the cost of Pampers. The amount of child support I received from Clinton was minimal. I was forced to do something I never thought I would do…. apply for welfare benefits.

I humbled myself and went to the public aid office to apply for benefits. I sat clenching my teeth as the caseworker asked one personal question after another. I was so embarrassed that I wanted to get up and walk out of that office but I didn't. I remember telling myself, "Sylvia you need the food stamps and the medical card." However, I made a promise to myself before I left that office that I would never put myself in a position where I would ever need public assistance again. I told myself that I would work for whatever I wanted in life and, Praise God, at this writing, I can proudly say that I have never been in a position of need since.

Although applying for welfare would be one of the most humiliating experiences I would have, it also would prove to be a blessing in disguise. It was apparent that I needed more education to care for my child. However, I had no idea where I would get the money for college tuition. Then a friend told me that, since I received public assistance, I could also be eligible for tuition benefits. I called my caseworker to find out if what my friend said was true and…it was. I'm glad I didn't walk out of the public aid office that day. Enduring the embarrassment was definitely worth the cost of tuition.

Finding Me after *It*

The effects of the violence I had witnessed went

deeper than just what I saw. The violence left behind negative, self-limiting emotions and feelings. I was plagued with low self-esteem and depleted self-confidence and often felt inferior to others. I found that I repeatedly told myself that I wasn't good enough. I would say, "You can't do that. Your grades weren't that good. Remember you have a baby." I would later learn that what I was doing was termed negative self-talk. I heard a quote once by former first lady, Eleanor Roosevelt, that says, "You must do the thing which you think you cannot do." I found strength in that saying; it became the mantra I used to push myself past those self-limiting thoughts.

After discovering I was eligible for tuition benefits, I contacted a university located in downtown Chicago. After a short phone conversation, I scheduled an appointment with an enrollment officer for the following day. When I arrived at the school the next day, I found it hard to go inside.

Before I could enter the building, my negative self-talk started and was non-stop:

"Girl, what in the world are you doing? People like you don't go to college."

"Who is going to take care of your son while you go to school?"

"Did you forget your final grades?"

As I pulled open the doors to the school, although I felt like I did during the days Mom was in court. I was trembling as I opened the door but I did it anyway. I enrolled in college at the age of twenty-four, several years after graduating high school. While I expected to struggle, in light of my high school grades and late enrollment, I was amazed that I actually did quite well. I passed all my classes the first semester and I astonished myself in the second semester.

I was terrified to speak in front of people – another effect of the violence I witnessed. In my second semester, I enrolled in a Public Speaking class. I felt I had to get over my fear of speaking and that class seemed to be the answer. The first day of class, I felt as if the instructor, Dr. Richardson, saw something in me that I didn't see in myself. In some ways, he seemed to be a combination of my father (who wanted more for me in life) and my friend who encouraged me to graduate. He called on me often during class, as if he knew I had this fear and needed his help to conquer it.

During the final weeks of class, Dr. Richardson gave an assignment that I believe helped me in more ways than one. The assignment was to write a report on a human interest topic that personally concerned us. It required that we do extensive research on the topic and include an outline, footnotes, list of resources, and a ten-minute classroom presentation. The topic I decided to write about was "Child Abuse." To this day, I can't say why I chose that topic. I mean, my siblings and I weren't physically abused, so there was really no connection. However, I would soon find out otherwise. While researching for the project, I learned that both children who are physically abused and children who witness violence are affected in similar ways.

Both display behaviors such as depression, poor school adjustment, low self-esteem, inferiority, shame, and guilt – to name a few. And although children who are physically abused carry visible signs of their abuse, both may have internal scarring. For the first time, I understood why I was plagued with the negative self-limiting feelings.

When it came time to deliver my presentation, I had everything I needed, except visuals. So after I delivered the report, I placed blank poster boards around the room and I asked the class if any of them had ever seen a victim of child abuse. It seemed that the whole class was answering and while they were either nodding or saying yes, I said, "Envision the face of that child, your victim, on one of these boards." I looked around the room then continued, "If it was your friend, envision your friend. If it was your brother or sister, envision the face of your brother or sister. If it was you, put your face on the board."

The emotion in the class was high. It seemed that all the students were affected in some way by my presentation. When I looked back at Dr. Richardson, he was smiling and clapping. I made the Dean's List that semester and I discovered that I wasn't alone. Even better, I was never plagued by the negative feelings of low self-esteem, low self-confidence and inferiority again. I went on to work as an Account Executive in sales at several major businesses often earning six-figure commissions, something that could never happen for a person afraid to talk and with feelings of inferiority. And, I accomplished that with a son.

"Though no one can go back and make a brand new start, anyone can start from now and make a brand new ending."

-Carl Bard

The Life Detox Coach

My time in Dr. Richardson's class did more than just confirm that my high school grades did not represent my potential. Because of the students' response to my presentation, I realized that we all go through something. In my book, The Journey Back to You, I write that everyone has a story – no one is exempt. Adversity does not look at our background or upbringing. It doesn't check our bank accounts or take into account where we live or what we drive. Adversity doesn't care where you work or how many figures are in the salary you're paid. Although our adverse experiences are relative to each of us, when it comes to adverse situations, no one is immune.

I once heard it said that we are the sum total of all we've ever experienced. Our life experiences create how we think, negative or positive. In turn, that way of thinking left unchecked does ultimately shape who we become. I realized that growing up in a violent atmosphere changed the course of my life. I went from being the dreamer who dreamed of a better life, to becoming someone who settled. And after I became pregnant, I became someone who couldn't see possibilities. I felt that life was over.

None of that was true. I was still the same dreamer, albeit with a child, but a dreamer nonetheless. And my experience in Dr. Richardson's class created a desire in me to move beyond my past to help others do the same. I went on to receive life coaching certification through the CaPP Institute's Certified Personal and Executive Coach program and I began a new journey.

Through my signature programs: **Life Detox Now Coaching and Be Made Whole Workshops**, I encourage and inspire people to let go of their past, live in their now and prepare for their future.

Attendees are taken through the WHOLE life process which helps them discover:

Who they are

How they think

Open up to possibilities

Let go and,

Expect the best.

You too can begin a new journey despite your past.

You, In Spite of It

By now, I hope you've grasped that my **It** was the violence I experienced as a child, not the fact that I had a child. Witnessing violence in my home opened the door for low self-esteem, guilt and shame which led to my lack of good judgment. In some ways, my pregnancy was my attempt at having some control over my life.

You may feel becoming pregnant and having a child at an early age or out of wedlock is your **It.** If so, you may also feel as though your life has changed and that whatever you thought you could do or would be prior to having a child is a distant thought. I urge you to consider this fact: life is not over for you. Though the course of your life may have changed, that doesn't mean the change has to be considered for the worse. How your story ends depends solely on you and your response to your new reality. Sure, it will take work and require time but it's not impossible. You will, however, have to change your thinking and rid yourself of any negative emotions or habits that have not served you and are not helpful for the life you desire.

Your circumstances do not define you or dictate what

your future will be; it is your willingness to change your response to the situation that will either propel you forward or cause you to remain stuck. The choice is yours. Regardless of the situation, you still have control over what your future will look like. Therefore, if you get anything out of this chapter, please get this: **if anyone ever overcame their past mistakes, difficulties or adversities and fulfilled their dreams, guess what? So can you!**

Here are four steps to help get you started:

1. **Forgive yourself.**

After my lapse in judgment, I began to question myself. I asked myself how could I have let it happen? With all I wanted for myself, I wondered, what was wrong with me that I allowed me to be in that situation?

2. **Remember your dreams.**

Although my pregnancy was unplanned and made an already difficult situation even more so, the truth was that unless I allowed it, my pregnancy should not have hindered my dreams. My pregnancy was not a death sentence to my dreams and neither is yours.

Surround yourself with cheerleaders.

My friend was right when she told me, "Having a child should not have changed what you had dreamed for yourself." Surround yourself with people who will encourage you to keep going and follow your dreams no matter what. If you don't have a friend who will stand by your side and cheer you on, consider me your friend and hear me when I say this: **You have everything inside you to accomplish the dreams you have for yourself, REGARDLESS OF YOUR PAST!**

3. **Stay Focused.**

Of course, realizing the dreams you have for yourself will require your utmost attention. The only thing between you and your dream is you. And, if you want it, you can have it. It is my hope that you will see that everything is possible.

As I end this chapter and my message to you, I hope you are encouraged to continue following the dreams you had before your pregnancy. Remember to first forgive yourself as it all starts with forgiveness. What happened, happened. Acknowledge it, accept it and move on. Second, remember your dreams. Remember what it was that you wanted for your life because it's still possible.

Third, the people you spend time with will either help

or hinder you. Surround yourself with people who have the same goals and desires. And lastly, stay focused. Be aware of the many traps that will be set to keep you from becoming the person you've dreamt of becoming. I've included coaching questions to jumpstart you into your new life. Be honest with yourself as you answer each question and remember... Don't Let **It** Stop You from becoming the person you were meant to be.

Life Detox Now Coaching Questions

Forgive yourself.

What is it that you need to forgive yourself for as it relates to your pregnancy?

_____

_____

_____

_____

Remember your dreams.

What was it that you aspired to be before you became pregnant? Explain why.

_____

_____

_____

_____

Surround yourself with cheerleaders.

Who is it that will support you unconditionally?

_____

_____

_____

_____

Pay it forward. Be a cheerleader to someone who needs you.

Sometimes, we help ourselves when we help others. Who can you support? How?

_____

_____

If you have experienced or been a witness to Domestic Violence, you are not alone. For more information about getting to safety, call your local Domestic Violence program. To find the closest program in your area, contact the 24-hour National Domestic Violence Hotline:

Voice: (800) 799-7233 (SAFE)
TTY: (800) 787-3244

If you are in immediate danger, call
911

If you need help from abuse
1(800) 25 ABUSE

In an effort to protect the privacy of my family and friends as well as others involved, names have been changed.

Alicia Bowens: I Forgave Me

"In order to heal we must first forgive…and sometimes the person we must forgive is ourselves."

-Mila Bron

Forgiveness is the key to your breakthrough. Without forgiveness, you remain attached to that event or decision, unable to move forward. Even as I am writing, I am wrestling with including this in the book because a lot of the things that I am about to share in this chapter I have only spoken about to a few.

The self-destructive effects of unforgiveness

In my previous book, L.O.V.E. for Teen Moms, I shared how I was able to graduate from high school, college, and obtain a successful career all while raising my son. However, there were situations that I encountered along the way that forced me to make some critical decisions, a few that I am not proud of. As these poor and shameful decisions would pile up, I would devalue myself less and less.

I became a mother at the age of fifteen. This was definitely a different space for me. Before then, I was an honor student at the top of my class, as well as a great athlete. I was the quiet girl. However, the thoughts and memories in my mind were quite loud.

I grew up in a family of strong, single women. Women who had the courage to get out of marriages full of infidelity, physical abuse, or drug abuse. They raised their children on their own and somehow kept things together. However, those women were left with emotional scars. Those failed relationships left them with nothing positive to say about the men that were once in their lives or men in general. I couldn't even begin to imagine how this must have made my uncles feel. As a result, I grew up with the perception that I shouldn't depend on a man for anything and that men could not be trusted.

I remember my father and mother being together up until I was about three. Then suddenly, my dad was no longer around. My questions of his whereabouts would go unanswered. Shortly after their split, my mother suffered an aneurysm, which left her paralyzed on her left side. My grandmother cared for my sister, who was only around nine months old at the time, and me while my mother recovered.

My two uncles, who also lived with my grandmother, became my father figures in my father's absence. A few years later my aunt remarried and I gained another uncle.

When I was about eight years old, we finally moved back into our old house, though my mom never did fully recover from the aneurysm. My great-grandmother and grandmother would come by to help my mom take care of things around the house. Soon I would take on many of those responsibilities, some of them being things that no nine or ten-year-old would normally do. Because of this, I would quickly develop into an independent kid.

By the time I reached my teenage years, all of my experiences had manifested into feelings of frustration and anger. From the outside, I was calm and quiet. However, years of learning to handle things and figure them out for myself caused me to internalize how I truly felt. I never felt I had anyone to confide in. As a result, feelings of anger and frustration began to manifest. I would often wonder why I couldn't just have a normal life. Why did *my* mom have to get sick? Why couldn't I have a normal mother and father like everyone else? The feelings of resentment I had towards my family turned into anger. Soon, sex became my outlet for this anger, and shortly thereafter I became a mother. *What self-destructive behaviors is an unforgiving spirit exhibiting in your life?*

Fueled by fire

Before I had my son, showing up at school at the beginning of my sophomore year was an eye-opening experience. I quickly learned who my real friends were. The feelings of shame, disappointment, and rejection just added fuel to the angry fire that was burning inside of me. When I returned to school after having my son, I came back with a vengeance. I no longer cared who did or didn't like me, I kept a small circle of friends, and I just did me. Yes, getting through high school and going to college was in my plans, but I was going to do it on my own terms.

I no longer strived to be at the top of my class or to be a top athlete. I did just enough to get by. Fortunately, the high grades and GPA that I achieved my first two years helped to buffer me from my lackluster performance of my junior and senior years.

If you play with fire...

It was my senior year of high school. I was with a

friend and we were on our way home from a concert when I met him. He caught my eye. He signaled for us to pull over. We did (thank God for protecting us from our foolishness). He was fine – caramel skin, curly hair, sparkling eyes. He had a friend with him. They asked us to follow them. We did (again, more foolishness). We followed them to their home in the city, chatted for a while outside, then exchanged numbers and continued our journey home. That was the beginning of a relationship that would teach me many hard lessons.

Soon after I started dating him, I began engaging in behaviors that could have very well cost me my future – staying out all night, missing school and work.

This new-found freedom was liberating to me. I never had a boyfriend that lived on his own. He was very much involved in the street life. He didn't work an honest job, but I didn't care. The fact that I had a place where I could get away from it all was enough for me.

...you'll get burned

Going to his house was like a drug to me. I went every chance I got, often leaving my mother or grandmother to care for my son. Unfortunately, it would soon become my prison.

One day, we were outside of his house, talking and playing around. He got a little carried away, playing as if he was going to throw me off the porch. I quickly got upset and cursed him out, so loudly that it caught the attention of the neighbors across the street. After that, we went inside and continued to argue about the incident. I was going to his room to get my things and go home. He was following behind me. When I turned around to face him, that's when it happened. He hit me.

Immediately I thought about all of the abusive relationships in my family. *This is not going to be my story,* I thought to myself. I heard my aunt's voice in my head telling me to never let a man put his hands on me. All of the anger began to boil up inside of me. *No way was he going to hit me and get away with it,* I thought to myself.

I started swinging my arms, determined to make sure he felt my anger and would know never to put his hands on me again. He caught my hands. He hit me again. Much harder. The sting of this blow lingered. I knew if I hit him again, his comeback would be worse. So I didn't. So many thoughts were running through my mind at that moment. I couldn't believe he hit me. I couldn't believe I allowed this to happen. I needed to get out of this relationship. I wanted to go home. He threatened to come to my house and kill me and my family if I left him or told anyone about this incident. So I stayed in the relationship.

A prisoner of my own freedom

Shortly after that incident, the verbal abuse began. Often he would tell me that if I left him, no one would want me. He also continued threatening to kill my family.

It's amazing how the adolescent mind works sometimes. I wanted out of this relationship. Though I had my doubts about him making good on his threats if I did leave him, I surely didn't want to find out. But more importantly, he was my prom date. If I left him now, who would I go to prom with? It was one month away. I had already backed out of one date for him. So I endured the relationship and made a promise to myself that I would leave him after prom. Silly girl.

My prom was a night that I don't mind forgetting. I worked as many hours as I could to save up money for my dress and tickets, but still had to end up borrowing money from my cousin to pay the balance on my dress. I couldn't afford to rent a car, so we took mine. On top of that, he was two hours late! By the time we made it to the venue, dinner was over, and people were already leaving. We only had time to take a few pictures and leave. After prom, we stopped at Church's to pick up a chicken dinner, then headed to his house. Night over.

A few weeks had passed since prom and now there was nothing holding me back from ending the relationship. I would be leaving for school in the fall, so I figured that would make the transition easier for me. I began to think of ways that I could end the relationship. *Maybe I'll use leaving for school as my reason? Maybe I can stop answering his calls?* Those all seemed to be viable options, but for some reason, I found myself still wanting to stay in the relationship. *Maybe things will be different? He hasn't hit me since that one incident.* While contemplating my decision, one thing would soon be missed – my period. The pregnancy test came back positive. Damn.

Desperate to get out

I didn't know what to do. How could I let this happen? I would be leaving for school in a few weeks. What was I going to do? How was I going to be able to care for *two* kids in school? So many questions raced through my head. Abortion was not an option. I didn't condone that. I didn't believe in it. There's no way I could ever give up my child for adoption. I couldn't bear the thought of someone else having my child. School was non-negotiable for me. No matter what I decided, I would still be attending college in the fall. I made the choice to keep the baby and take time off if needed, when the baby came. I also decided to stay with him. *Maybe things will be better now,* I thought to myself. Yeah, right.

Outside of the verbal abuse, things seemed to go well for the next few weeks. I had lucked up and found an affordable apartment right off campus, and I was working and saving up money for my move, which was coming up very quickly. I still hadn't told my family about my pregnancy. I decided to wait until I started showing. It was still really early anyway.

As the time grew closer to my leaving, he began to

make comments expressing his discontentment with my leaving, saying things like *You're going to go down there and forget about me* – asking me if I was sure I wanted to go. Going to college was the one thing that I was sure of. His questions would soon turn to insecurities, then the verbal abuse increased, then making threats that I better not be thinking about seeing anyone else or he'd beat me and the other guy's asses. I ignored him, but assured him that *that* wouldn't happen. I couldn't wait to get out of there.

The big day was now a few weeks away. I was still working, trying to save up as much money as I could for my move and my security deposit on my place. One morning, I let him use my car so that he could run some errands while I was at work. Then he was going to pick me up when I got off.

It was a good day. I was at the top of the board for sales. This paycheck was going to be a good one. The day drew to an end, so I called him to let him know that I would be getting off soon. While I was waiting for him to arrive, I was having a conversation with a coworker. We were talking about school, career aspirations, and things of that nature. I then mentioned my friend to him, who also worked there, and suggested that he consider taking her out. She had mentioned to me that she liked him, so I thought I'd play matchmaker.

I was in the middle of telling him more about her when my boyfriend walked in. My heart dropped. I already knew what he was thinking by the expression on his face. I was scared. I quickly got up and walked to the car with him, explaining what we were talking about. He was quiet the entire ride. Once we made it to his house, he began to speak, angrily stating that I had no business talking to that guy. He didn't care what the reason was. He did not want me talking to *any* guys about anything. He was going to teach me not to talk to them. He led me to the basement of the house. He hit me. Twice. Hard.

That was it for me. I knew I didn't want to be tied to him for the rest of my life. I couldn't have a child with him and allow it to experience having an abusive parent. I didn't want my children to go through what my mother and her siblings went through, especially seeing how it affected them as adults. I decided to have an abortion. I soon made my appointment to have it done.

As I sat in the clinic waiting for my name to be called,

everything inside of me wanted to run out of that building. Finally, they called my name and led me to the back. They started me on an IV, then began the procedure. I lay there and cried as the sound of the vacuum, suctioning, and cutting took my baby away. Finally, it was over. It was done.

Inviting misery back

The day had finally come. Move-in day at school. A fresh start. I was still sad that I had ended my pregnancy, but happy to have ended my relationship with him. I was optimistic about what these next few years of college life would bring. New friendships. New relationships. Graduation. A successful career and better life for me and my son.

A few weeks passed. The excitement of my new journey had faded away. Now there was just me in this foreign place with hardly any friends. Since I lived off campus, making new friends was a challenge. All of the freshmen were living in the dorms. One of my high school friends was also attending the same college but I didn't want to cramp his style. My older sister was also there but she lived in an apartment across town and I was sure she would have no interest attending any freshmen events.

I was allowing myself to get situated and adjusted before I brought my son down, so not even he was there to keep me busy. Homesickness quickly began to come over me. I needed to connect to something familiar to me. So I called him. The calls were infrequent at first, then increased in frequency as time passed, to the point where we were talking every day. As much as I didn't want him back in my life, I kept inviting him in. *What things or people do you keep inviting back into your life that shouldn't be there?*

Before I knew it, he was back in my life and in my apartment. An altercation in his neighborhood had lead to him getting shot. Even though I knew I shouldn't be involved with him, I still cared about him. So I invited him to come down and stay with me.

A prisoner…again

The end of the semester was fast approaching. It had been a few months since he moved in. He was enrolled in classes to get his GED and even found a job. However, the verbal abuse and threats of physical abuse picked right back up when he arrived.

It's amazing how the mind works because when the

verbal abuse initially began, I would ignore it and my mind did not accept those words. However, as time passed I actually found myself believing the things he said. Negative words work just like affirmations. If you keep hearing or saying negative things about yourself, then you will indeed slowly begin to believe them. That's why it is important to surround yourself with people who lift you up and speak life into you.

When I went to campus, I avoided interacting with males as much as I could, even dressing down and neglecting to comb my hair to ensure they didn't notice me. I avoided social events at all costs. I didn't want to do anything that would cause him to think that I was seeing or even talking to any other guys.

I soon began to feel like I was a prisoner in my own home. I wanted him gone and out of my life. I began to fantasize about ways to get him to leave…or disappear. Like a caged animal desperately wanting its freedom, my mind went into survival mode. On campus, we often received free sample items such as sleeping pills and No Doze, amongst many other things. I always kept them around just in case I needed them, so I had a drawer full. One particular day, while I was fixing him some oatmeal, there was a packet of sleeping pill samples still laying on the counter. *I could take all of the packets of sleeping pills, crush them, put them in his oatmeal, and let him go to sleep forever,* I thought to myself. *There's no way anyone would find out. I could get away with it.* At that point it all made sense. It seemed like all of the logic in my mind had been cut off. Suddenly, it was as if I was having an out of body experience. I was looking at myself standing in the kitchen staring at the oatmeal and pills. I felt God was showing me myself. *Is this what I had become? Is this who I wanted to be?* No. I had to get out of this relationship. God, help me.

The final straw

Finals were less than a month away. I had taken my son back to Chicago so that I could focus on studying. I still hadn't worked up the nerve to break up with him, and there was no way I was going to involve anyone else in my drama. I wasn't sure what he was capable of and I didn't want my family or friends getting hurt because of me.

A few days later, a friend of mine called to see if I could give him a ride to the cleaners. Obviously, my boyfriend was not having that. In no way was I going to give any guy a ride anywhere; he didn't care who it was. The argument escalated to the point of him raising his hand as if he was going to hit me. I walked away from him. His voice grew louder and angrier. Suddenly he was coming behind me. I ran out of the apartment, screaming.

There I was outside, with no keys or phone. I began walking. I had no idea where I was going at the moment – I just needed to get away from there. *I can't do this anymore,* I thought to myself. I decided to walk across town to my sister's. I was going to tell her everything that was going on, then come back and get him out of my apartment. I made it to her place and knocked on the door. No answer. She wasn't there. I left her place and continued to walk around.

A few hours had now passed. I decided to head back home. I was going to have to handle this on my own. There was no way that I could continue in a relationship like this. Even if I had to fight my way out, it was going to end today. As I approached my place, I prayed to God, asking for Him to protect me and help me find the words to say to end this relationship.

I slowly made my way up the stairs to my place. I entered the door and saw him sitting in the bedroom. I made my way back there and sat next to him. I took a deep breath, continuing to pray as I sat there.

"I can't do this anymore," I said as calmly as I could. "I cannot continue to be in a relationship where I am not trusted."

I told him that he needed to be gone by the end of the semester. His response was surprisingly calm. He apologized, told me how much he loved me, and said a few other things, most of which I tuned out. My mind was made up. Nothing could be said that would change my decision.

As the semester drew to a close, he did slowly begin to move his things out and I would learn that I was pregnant again. This time, I didn't tell him. I quickly made an appointment and had it taken care of. By the end of the semester, he was completely out of my life. Now it was time for me to get back to the basics: focusing on my son and my education.

Picking up the pieces

My second semester in college began with me being on academic probation. All of the drama from the first semester had definitely interfered with my studies, and as a result, my grades were barely passing. However, I was determined to make it through college. There was no way I was going back home without a degree. I needed that to make life better for me and my son.

Relationships were the farthest thing from my mind at that time. I knew that I wasn't emotionally ready to be involved with anyone. I needed time to heal. It would be about a year before I even began to date again.

Throughout the course of the next three years, I connected with other young mothers on campus, gained new friendships, became actively involved in campus life, and raised my son – watching him grow from a young toddler to graduating from kindergarten. I also graduated.

No compromising

Finding a job after college was a challenge. However, with a little consistency and persistence, I was able to get a job in my field. This was before applying for jobs online became the norm, so every morning I would look for jobs that were in my field on job sites, company websites, and the classifieds, and I would spend my mornings faxing off and emailing my resumes.

It took me six months after graduation to finally land a job in my field. During those six months, I worked a few temporary jobs to bring in some income, but I stayed committed to getting the job that I wanted. I was also back at home with my mom, so that made it a lot easier for me to take the time to find what I really wanted. There were plenty of times I wanted to throw in the towel and just take whatever job I could find, but I knew that would not help my career path. I didn't want to get stuck in a field that I didn't want to be in. This taught me the importance in not compromising what it is that you want.

What goals or dreams do you have that you have compromised?

The cycles continue

Although I was beginning to get my life together professionally, I was still failing in the relationship area. Over and over again I would find myself involved in relationships with guys that weren't looking for commitment. One relationship resulted in me having my second son. Another after that resulted in yet a third abortion. I was losing myself in these relationships –giving up so much of myself and left empty.

After having my second son, I decided to go back to school and obtain my master's degree so that I could further my career. I also purchased my first home. Everything seemed to be going in the right direction. Why was I having so much trouble finding a good relationship?

The wakeup call

Three years had passed since I moved into my new home. I had obtained my MBA and was completing a second master's degree. I advanced my career by finding a better paying job with more opportunities for growth. My oldest son was now in junior high and doing well. My youngest was now three.

I was happy in my job but felt that there was more that I was called to do. I knew that there had to be more for me than just waking up and going to work for the next 30 or so years. So I became involved with and volunteered for several organizations.

Then suddenly, my grandmother passed. The one who stepped in and helped raise me and my sister when my mother got sick. The one who always told me that she was proud of me and never hesitated to brag about me. The one whom I depended heavily on to help me care for my children, whether it was caring for them while I was at work, or if I just needed a break. I felt I lost everything when I lost her. She was my security blanket. She was the one who made me feel like everything was going to be ok. Now she was gone. All of that was gone.

I began throwing myself into more activities and more empty relationships, and neglecting my children. I was emotionally and spiritually depleted. Eventually my oldest would begin acting out, a sure cry for attention, and a turning point for me. I needed to get my priorities in order, and the first priority was my children. But I knew I wouldn't be able to do this by myself...I needed God. ***Have you experienced any wakeup calls in your life? If so, how did you respond?***

The glass ceiling of an unforgiving spirit

My oldest son was now in high school. I removed myself from all of the empty relationships and started devoting more time to him and his activities, with my youngest right by my side. I also began attending church regularly and volunteering there as well. As I began to develop a deeper relationship with God, He began to reveal things to me about myself that I had not noticed before. I had some serious issues. The majority of those issues were rooted in not forgiving others and most importantly myself.

Being unforgiving was wreaking havoc in my life. In every aspect of my life, I felt I would never get beyond a certain level of achievement. It was limiting my potential. It was keeping me from having the type of relationship that I so desired. It was stunting my career. It was keeping me from my purpose. I once heard someone say that you cannot receive with a closed fist. It was time for me to let go of my past and all of the hurt in it and forgive so that I could get to my next level.

Who do you need to forgive? What past hurts do you need to let go of?

The healing begins

Sometimes the hardest thing you can do is forgive. I often found myself dwelling in the land of "what if" – always wondering how my life would be different if someone else or I had made different choices. My disappointment those choices were ultimately my condemnation of myself and them.

Forgiving others meant that I would have to accept the decisions and actions that others took in the past and understand that they did what they could, based on where they were emotionally, spiritually, and physically at that time. What I would have done if I were them was not applicable, because they were not me and did not think exactly like me. I had to accept that I could not control what people do, but I could control me.

Having a child was just a symptom of a bigger problem going on with me. Although I was smart, I had been an angry and insecure teenager who was not happy with my circumstances. I was upset that I didn't have a normal mom like everyone else and I blamed her for getting sick. I was angry about my father not being in my life. I was angry about always having to figure things out on my own.

It was time for me to come to terms with these issues and forgive. I came to the realization that some things that happened in my life were beyond everyone's control but, in fact, were blessings to me in the end. My mother getting sick prepared me for my early parenthood by helping me become more responsible and independent. My father's absence taught me the importance of making sure my children's fathers were a part of their lives, whether or not we were together. Everything that I had experienced was simply preparing me for my future and for that I was grateful.

However, the biggest issue that I still had was with forgiving myself. There were so many decisions that I made in my past that I didn't forgive myself for. One by one, I began to forgive myself for:

Repeating cycles. I forgave myself for repeating the generational cycles of single parenthood and abusive relationships.

The abortions. I forgave myself for going against my beliefs and allowing fear to control my actions. I understand that I made the best decision I could based on where I was emotionally and spiritually at the time.

Devaluing myself. I forgave myself for devaluing myself in my relationships and professional life. I misrepresented myself to others and sabotaged my own growth. I now knew my worth and would never sabotage my success or settle again.

The possibilities are endless

Although being a teen mom was an obstacle, the greatest obstacle that I had to overcome was myself and my unforgiving mindset. I had allowed that angry, insecure teenager to run my life and I was only able to tame her and regain control by forgiving and accepting both myself and my past.

Now, my life has gone to levels that I have never experienced. I have a great career and earn the money that I deserve. I've started a few of my own businesses that are in alignment with my purpose and generating income. I am connected to networks of powerful people who are dedicated to walking in their purpose and helping others do the same. My children are thriving. And I have an amazing man who not only loves me but prays with and for me. There were still some challenges I faced along the way and I'm sure more will come. But having a forgiving and positive mindset helps to navigate the obstacles much easier.

In closing, I hope that through all of the stories shared in this book, if you only get one thing, know that in spite of whatever it is you have gone (or are going through), there is still a fortune inside of you. You are loved more than you may realize and worth more than you may recognize.

Regardless of your circumstances or past, you are still pregnant with great, *planned* purpose. Someone in this world is waiting for you to realize – and walk in – your greatness. Even if it takes longer than planned, don't give up on your dreams. Push past the doubts, shame, and fears, and unleash your fortune because the world needs you. You ARE a Millionaire M.O.M.!

Millionaire *M.O.M.* Challenge #4

"Forgiveness is about empowering your-self, rather than empowering your past."

-Bishop T.D. Jakes

In order to be able to move on and embrace our future, we must first let go of our past. Letting go involves forgiveness – of others or even ourselves. Think of someone you have been struggling to forgive. Write a letter describing how their actions made you feel. Then conclude it by releasing them of all wrongdoing and forgiving them. Burn the letter as a symbol of your release.

Reflect on the following questions:

1. How did writing the letter make you feel?

2. How did you feel after burning the letter?

V. I Am a Millionaire M.O.M

"You were put on this earth to achieve your greatest self, to live out your purpose, and to do it courageously."

— Steve Maraboli

I am a mother on a mission to unleash my fortune. I am determined to release everything God has placed inside of me to help change the lives of others. I change the trajectory of my own life by combating any beliefs or habits that I have developed throughout the course of my life that can hinder me from reaching my destiny. I defy the standards placed on me and have redefined my new normal. I know that I am more than enough and am fully capable of creating the wealth I desire.

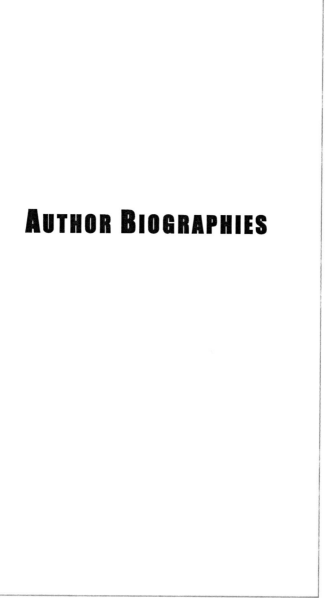

AUTHOR BIOGRAPHIES

Chandra Pointer
Da Urban Girl's Mentor

Chandra Pointer: wife, honored mother of three gifted daughters, nurse, mentor, and entrepreneur is the founder and executive director of SisterNation Inc., a non-profit mentoring program that promotes sisterhood by way of mentoring group sessions, life skills workshops, community service projects, and social and cultural outings. Sister-Nation also advocates against sexual victimization of girls.

Chandra started SisterNation, Inc. 4 years ago in Harvey, Illinois in the community room of the Bethlehem Village Apartments after struggling with her own teenage daughter for years and discovering that many of her female family members, including herself, had been victims of sexual abuse, struggling with low self-esteem, and battling depression.

Chandra is currently working on her first book titled,

Mommy Issues, in which she shares her struggles with her mother and how mothers and daughters can work together to build strong genuine and authentic relationships during turbulent adolescent times.

Chandra lives in Hazel Crest, Illinois with her supportive husband and beautiful daughters.

"When a girl feels loved and valued, she makes wise decisions and those decisions create a better life for her."

Sisterhood is powerful! *~Chandra...Sister*
Love

Connect with Chandra:

Facebook: Chandra Nicole

Da Urban Girl's Mentor

SisterNation

Web: www.sisternation.org

www.daurbangirlsmentor.com

Email: chandrapointer@sisternation.org

daurbangirlsmentor@gmail.com

Corita Key

The Innovator

Corita Key is the proud mother of five young children. She had her first child at the age of seventeen but refused to let her status as a teenage mother stop her from achieving her dreams.

Corita graduated from Triton College with an Associate's Degree in Science and earned her Bachelor of Social Work from Governors State University. She is the 2015 recipient of The Dr. Margaret T. Burroughs Scholarship and a proud member of the Phi Alpha Honor Society for Social Work.

Corita is the founder of a non-profit organization which helps build strong educational foundations to change negative social behaviors in children. She believes many of the images in the media were a strong influence on her during her teen years and contributed to her becoming a teen mom. She wants to help other teenage girls avoid similar traps. "Those images distracted me. I want girls to know that there is a difference between what's in those magazines and what's reality," she says.

Corita devotes much of her free time to volunteering at her children's school and throughout her community of Maywood, where she aspires to one day be elected mayor.

Connect with Corita:

Facebook: Key Corita

Dorothea Cooper
The Legacy Protector

Dorothea Cooper-Jackson became a teenage mother at the age of sixteen and is now a proud single mother of four children. Faced with single parenthood at an early age, this south side Chicago native did not let that stop her from pursuing her dreams. In 2000, she completed her high school education and went on to study Networking and Communications at Devry University where she graduated with a Bachelor's degree in 2003. She enrolled in Keller Graduate School of Management, where she was an honors student, and in 2007, she obtained her Master's in Business Administration. She has been a member of the Business Honor Society since 2007.

Dorothea works at HERE Maps LLC, where she supervises data distribution for Americas and Asia Pacific regions. In 2015, she became a certified life insurance producer and now helps families protect themselves and secure their future with life insurance and physical gold acquisition. Dorothea has a passion for helping others and commits her time to mentoring and educating young adults in money management and career development.

Through her work with Chicago Cares Inner City Community Development, she helps others develop their own leadership potential and transform their lives.

Dorothea's personal experiences have taught her to be persistent and tenacious, and each day she lives her mantra, "If there's a will, God has already made a way."

Connect with Dorothea:

Website: www.dottieofgold24karatbars.com
Email: dottieofgold@gmail.com

Luberta Lytle
The Mind Changer

Luberta Lytle is the owner and Founder of LL Life Coaching Company. She is a Certified Christian Life Coach, Motivational Speaker, and Mentor. She helps women who are stuck and unsatisfied in their current career and life paths find fulfillment by activating and implementing their purpose. Luberta received her Bachelor of Science in Organizational Leadership from Greenville College in Greenville and her Master of Business Administration from Lindenwood University in Belleville, Illinois.

Luberta works as a qualified intellectual disabilities professional for the State of Illinois. She has worked for the State of Illinois for twenty-eight years. She also worked under the following job titles: mental health technician, licensed practical nurse, residential service supervisor, and public service administrator.

Luberta is a longstanding member of AFSCME Union Local 401, where she has held numerous roles including President, Vice-President, Executive Board Member and Trustee. She is very active in several community and professional organizations including Sisters Influencing Sisters (S.I.S.), a non-profit which offers mentoring, self-esteem building, and self-confidence development for young ladies in grades five through twelve. She is also a member of the Matrons Women Club, the Black Women Networking Organization, and sits on the board of the Centralia Community Youth Center. Luberta lives in Centralia, Illinois with her husband Delmore. When she is not working, this mother of three, likes to travel, read, and enjoy time with her eleven grandchildren.

Connect with Luberta:

Website: www.lubertalytle.com
Booking: lubertalytle.youcanbook.me
Email: lubertalytle@gmail.com
Phone: (209)732-6624
Facebook: Coach Luberta
Twitter: @luberta_lytle
Instagram: @mslytle

LaKeisha Stringfellow
The Women's Marketplace Mentor

LaKeisha is a caring, loving, strong, virtuous woman, with a heart to serve God and love people. Her background and experience include work at St. Francis Hospital in Blue Island, IL (now MetroSouth), as well as The University of Chicago Medical Center. Throughout her career, she has helped people find the necessary resources to better their health and communicate their needs to their primary care physician.

LaKeisha leads and mentors teenage girls in her local church community and makes sure they have a safe environment to share their concerns and struggles. She also serves as overseer of the Women of Wise, a local group affiliated with the Victorious Living Church of God. She hosts a weekly prayer line every second Saturday of the month called "Powerful Prayer Call," which uplifts and encourages women all over the U.S. LaKeisha speaks at events across the country, empowering and inspiring women of all social and economic levels.

Her overall mission is to be a catalyst for positive change by encouraging and uplifting others to live a healthy and prosperous life.

When LaKeisha is not out serving others, she enjoys spending time with her husband and children.

Connect with LaKeisha:

Website: www.lakeishastringfellow.com
Email: powerfulprayercall@gmail.com

Conchetta Jones
The Dreambuilder

Conchetta A. Jones is the Founder and CEO of *She's All That!* a personal development and mentoring organization for girls in grades three through twelve. She is also the Founder and Owner of *She's All That! Woman*, a Lifestyle Coaching Company for women who are ready to live a life of abundance as they follow their dreams. A graduate of Governors State University, she holds a Master's Degree in Communication and Training. Conchetta is a Certified Overflow Life Coach, a Certified Consumer Wellness Advocate, a model, model coach, speaker and author. Her books *I'm Doing It!* and *Dreamlife Journal*, help readers to work through their procrastination and begin to follow their dreams. Conchetta has had a very diversified career in her quest to follow her dreams. She has worked as a media specialist, reading teacher, an accounts receivable clerk, and a model. She currently works as a Product Program Manager for the Girl Scouts of Greater Chicago and Northwest Indiana.

Conchetta serves as Vice President of the National Association of Professional Women (NAPW), Orland Park Chapter and is a member of the Leadership Team for the NAPW, Chicago Chapter. She is also a board member and the Mentoring Chair for the Professional Women's Network (PWN)

During her spare time, Conchetta loves to read, write and spend time with her family and friends.

Connect with Conchetta:

Website: www.satwoman.com
Email: info@satwoman.com
Facebook: Conchetta Jones

Shettima Webb

Self-Esteem Advocate

Shettima Webb is a professional plus-size model, actress, writer, media personality, singer, songwriter, and poet, but the title she wears most proudly is Mother. Shettima gave birth to her son at just nineteen years old. At the age of twenty-six, she earned her Bachelor's Degree in Accounting Business and Finance, becoming the first college graduate in her immediate family.

While working as a corporate accountant, Shettima pursued her dream of being an actor and a model. In 2009, she won the Miss Illinois Plus America Pageant and went on to place 5th in the national pageant. Shettima has worked on several national print campaigns and became the first plus-size cover model for Allezom International Magazine. She is currently signed to Gill Hayes Talent Agency and YJB

Talent and has toured across the country as an actress with the Black Social Network. Shettima has been featured in major publications such as Essence, N'Digo, and Rolling Out, and has modeled on CAN-TV, WCIU-TV. She has graced runways in Chicago and at New York Fashion Week.

Shettima started Model Esteem, a performance arts company for youth and adults with a core focus in building self-esteem and anti-bullying through modeling and creative arts. Model Esteem has been featured on the local news, in print publications and on main stages such as the Daley Center and The Black Women's Expo in Chicago. Shettima is also the founder and host of Mocha Chocolate TV. Knowing all too well how bullying can damage one's self-esteem, Shettima uses her media skills and performance background to help others recognize their own value, learn to love themselves and appreciate their God-given beauty on the inside and out.

Shettima has been featured on WVON, Rejoice 102.3 and has hosted her own radio show on Intellectual Radio and TV Show on Can-TV.

She has also had the pleasure of being an interviewer at Steve Harvey's Neighborhood Award in Atlanta where she interviewed various well-known celebrities.

To reach Shettima about Modeling and Performance Arts, please go to www.modelesteem.com

Melanie Foote-Davis

Self-Love Coach and Freedom Catalyst

Melanie Foote- Davis is an author, self-love coach and freedom catalyst. As President of The Love and Freedom Academy, she helps women who are burdened with stress, overwhelm, shame and guilt find a place of unimaginable peace. She provides tools to align self-love and self-care with desired dreams to live a fulfilling and purposeful life.

Her expertise and gentle, yet no-nonsense approach leads women to breakthroughs that position them for lifelong success.

Melanie is on a mission to arm women and teen girls with the skills to reach their desired destination, unapologetically saying, "Yes," to themselves, "Yes," to their heart's desires and "Yes," to living a radically bold and courageous life.

272

Melanie has been featured on Fox 32 News, Smooth Jazz 90.5 FM HD, TEW Radio, EmPowered to Radio, and Rejoice 102.3 FM Radio.

In her free time, Melanie enjoys date nights with her husband, Sean, spa days, long walks, hiking, quiet evenings and quality time with family and friends. She embraces her corny side, laughs at her own jokes, and savors the silly moments in life.

Connect with Melanie:

Websites: RadicalLoveNotes.com

RadicalLoveBook.com

MelanieFooteDavis.com

Dr. Catrina Pullum

The Chain Breaker

Wife, mother, servant, vision coach, educator, mentor, advocate, and film & theatrical producer. While all of these titles describe Dr. Trina Pullum, when it comes to her life story, there's one title that stands out above them all: The Chain Breaker. Having overcome many challenges and trials that would have taken most out, Dr. Pullum encourages and inspires others through her testimony and thought-provoking workshops.

Her life's mission is to help women heal and grow their greatness. Dr. Pullum is the founder of RARE Inc., an organization dedicated to empowering young women through training and personal development, using practical and biblical principles. She serves as the board chair of Center of Empowerment for Families & Youth, Inc., a non-profit dedicated to helping low-income and at-risk families. Dr. Pullum serves as one of the Executive Officers of PullCorp Media & Business Consulting Group where she specializes in artist management, music production, public relations, and business consulting. As CEO of Puissance Maison Productions, Dr. Pullum has produced & directed several commercials, movies, and plays. She also serves as an International Officer for the Full Gospel Baptist Fellowship.

A New Orleans native and Tulane University Alumni, Dr. Pullum has been recognized for her life's work with proclamations from the House of Representatives, the Office of Mayor, and President Barack Obama.

Connect with Dr. Trina:

PullCorp Media Group
Phone: (225)366-7855
Email: pmg@pullcorp.com
Website: www.drcatrinapullum.com

Sylvia Duncan
The Life Detox Coach

Sylvia Duncan, The Life Detox Coach, is an author and inspirational speaker, helping people clear the clutter of "emotional toxicity" from their past to live a life that's happy and whole. As founder of The Duncan Approach and creator of *Life Detox Now* coaching and *Be Made Whole* workshops, she offers a series of life-changing programs that teach destiny seekers how to move past their pain and live with resilience.

A surviving witness of domestic violence, Sylvia believes that what we've experienced and overcome is meant to be shared to help others realize their purpose in life. In her home, the often used statement, *"What happens in this house, stays in this house"* kept her trapped in an emotional prison of what she refers to as "noisy silence." Although the violence was never talked about, the effects of what she experienced manifested into self-limiting emotions and behaviors that kept her stuck, such as low self-esteem and low self-confidence. For years, the unaddressed emotions were a constant reminder of her past. After discovering a way to successfully break past these *destiny stealers* and live the life she desired, she developed a series of programs to help others successfully walk in their destiny.

Through her *Life Detox Now* and *Be Made Whole* programs, Sylvia encourages men and women who are *Destiny Seekers* to free themselves from what's really holding them back; move past their past and come into the life they deserve.

She is the author of *The Journey Back to You,* a testimonial journey through adversity. Readers have appreciated the transparent message of hope she provides in showing that one's past can become a meaningful building block to their future.

Sylvia received professional and executive coach training and certification from the CaPP Institute, domestic violence training through Family Rescue and speaker training from the National Speakers Association's NSA-IL

Speaker Academy. She has appeared as a columnist for The Neighbor newspaper, The Straight No Chaser show on Intellectual Radio with Ria Rai Harris, and the Let's Stay Together show with Rick and Brenda McCain.

Visit www.sylviaduncan.com, and download your free copy of: **7steps** *to become a Successful Destiny Seeker*

Connect with Sylvia:

Facebook: Sylvia Duncan

Periscope: @SylviaDuncan

Twitter: @lifedetoxcoach

Email: dapproach@theduncanapproach.com

Phone: (773)991-5771

Tanya Winfield
Lifestyle Coach

Tanya Winfield beat out 250,000 prospective contestants to become one of the last six finalists on season 15 of NBC's weight-loss reality show, The Biggest Loser. Winfield – a top fan favorite – may not have won the big check, but she's won something even more valuable: she won a new, healthy lifestyle that have changed her life forever. Her journey and her story has inspired millions to begin fighting for their own healthy lifestyle – and she couldn't be more thankful.

Winfield is the first to admit that her experience on the show was as much a far cry from the lifestyle she'd grown accustomed to as anyone can get. Often referred to as the "people's champ," throughout the season, Winfield's impressive 87-lb weight loss advanced her to the final week of the competition as one of the last six contestants competing on the show.

Initially, her drive and determination to not let obesity win made her a top fan favorite but her vulnerability – when she opened up and shared the innermost details of her life – was the turning point in her journey. It served to deepen her connection with viewers across the nation who witnessed her breakthrough.

Winfield's raw recollection of her gruesome, childhood experience at the hands of an abusive, drug-addicted mother and a family who failed to come to her rescue was a personal tipping point in her journey. The heartbreaking memory she shared with her trainer on the show also became known as "The Most Inspiring Moment" in Biggest Loser history.

Winfield's phenomenal weight loss success is just one more extraordinary accomplishment that she has already achieved in her life begun anew. She also earned her first million dollars by the time she was thirty-five years old, as an entrepreneur, restaurateur, and corporate leadership/management executive with Fortune 500 companies during her 20-year tenure in corporate America. Becoming COO of an iconic Chicago franchise is yet another triumph in Winfield's life. However, all of these achievements are only a taste of what's to come for this fearless woman of excellence.

A proponent of quality, empowerment, distinction and now forgiveness, this teen mother has shed emotional baggage that far outweighs any pounds she's lost. Her pride in her personal victories comes in second to her determination to follow where this new path is leading her. Along with plans to release a cookbook, open healthy soul food franchises and spin clubs across the nation, Winfield's new path is all about sharing her message of hope and inspiration.

Winfield is proud to be a beacon of encouragement, inspiration, motivation, and transformation to anyone who needs a little light to break down the barriers set up by the mind and often obeyed by the body.

To that little girl who may be thinking she'll never amount to anything because of her upbringing, or that young woman who needs a little motivation to push past the challenges she's facing in her business; or the millions of people who don't believe they can lose weight because "It's just too hard," Winfield's message is simple, yet passionate: *Lose your emotional baggage in order to win your life back – because you are worth saving.*

Connect with Tanya:

Website: www.tanyawinfield.com

Alicia Bowens
Visionary Expert

Alicia Bowens is a woman of many talents. A self-proclaimed corpora-preneur, she is an IT professional by day and a sought after speaker, coach and radio host outside of her 9-to-5. A certified life coach, she is the founder of two businesses, BE IT LLC, an IT staffing and consulting company, and BE LOVE LLC, a company which connects teen and single moms to resources, education, and information through books, coaching, and workshops.

A 2015 Crown Jewel Award recipient and 2016 Boss Influencer, Alicia has been a frequent guest on a number of radio and TV shows and at events where she speaks about career planning, entrepreneurship, vision boards, relationships, and her experience being a teenage mother.

Alicia became a teen mom while attending high school in the south suburbs of Chicago, but she was determined to continue her education. After graduating, she attended the University of Illinois at Urbana-Champaign, taking her then three-year-old son with her. She earned her Bachelor's Degree in 2001 and began a career in the IT industry. In 2006, Alicia obtained her Masters in Business Administration and Masters in Information Systems Management from Keller Graduate School. Alicia is an active member of the national Black MBA Association Chicago Chapter, having served on the executive board and marketing and communications committee from 2006-2010. She also participated in the organization's Leaders of Tomorrow program, a mentorship program for high school students. Alicia has been involved in other teen mentoring programs such as the Legacy Initiative and Your Time Is Now (YTIN) and she volunteers with the Illinois Subsequent Pregnancy Program.

In 2010 Alicia became a certified life coach and now shares her experiences – both successes and failures – in an effort to empower others to achieve their goals despite their obstacles. As co-host of the LOVE Perspective Radio Show, Alicia provides a platform where others can be inspired and encouraged to live their dreams. Alicia believes that if you have a vision for your life, God has already instilled within you the skills and abilities that you need in order to make that vision a reality.

Connect with Alicia:

Website: www.aliciabowens.com
Facebook: Author Alicia Bowens
Twitter: @alicia_bowens
Instagram: @alicia_bowens
Periscope: @alicia_bowens
Phone: (855)254-2421

Millionaire *M.O.M.* Challenge #5

> *"You can waste your lives drawing lines, or you can live your life crossing them."*
>
> -*Shonda Rhimes*

Fulfilling your dreams requires you to step outside of your comfort zone. You must be willing to think differently, believe in your vision, and move in faith of what can be instead of how things are. Reach out and connect with one of the authors of this book. Schedule a meeting with them to discuss how they can help you move closer to pursuing your dreams.

Join the movement:

www.iamamillionairemom.com

CPSIA information can be obtained
at www.ICGtesting.com
Printed in the USA
FFOW02n0433081116
29148FF

9 781513 611846